PICKLES AND MILHOUS FLY AGAIN

YET ANOTHER POCKETFUL OF FUNNY TRUE-LIFE
STORIES

ERIC V. LITSKY

ERIC V. LITSKY

Paperback: 979-8-9883776-8-9

eBook: 979-8-9883776-9-6

Book Cover by Arlene Soto, Intricate Designs

Formatting and Publishing Consulting by Bannon River Books, LLC

First Edition

To Emerson, Grant, Zoe, and Juno.
My smart and beautiful grandchildren
who have inspired me to write my books.
I love you more than life itself.

ALSO BY ERIC V. LITSKY

Harry Would Be So Proud
Frying Pork Chops Naked

Available in print and e-book.
Also available in audiobook format.

For more information. www.EricLitsky.com

CONTENTS

PROLOGUE

This is my third book. Each of them is filled with heartwarming and funny stories from my life. Yes. I write about the stuff I've done. Places I've been. And people I've met along the way.

The good. The bad. And of course the ugly. I like unvarnished truth. It is far more interesting than parsing one's words.

My writing career began like most things in my life. Without a plan. Or a goal.

After I blew 70 candles out on my Carvel ice cream cake – don't try to fool me with a Baskin Robbins – I came to the realization that I've reached the age to become the keeper of my family's stories.

During the pandemic, I had way too much time on my hands. I began to write about my family. I thought my children and grandchildren needed to know about those who came before them.

I realized that my four grandchildren would never take the time to sit by my side and listen to stories from my life and the lives of family members long gone. They are too busy being kids. And kids don't have much patience listening to the stories of *old farts* like me. But these stories are rich with texture and self-deprecating humor.

If I have one regret, I wish I'd spent more time learning about the life and times of my grandparents. The oral history of one's family does fade with time. Once the keepers of the stories are gone, those stories are gone forever.

As I wrote I discovered that the stories about my life and times are not that much different from others. And that they are relevant and entertaining to those of any age or background.

I'll apologize in advance as some of my stories are sprinkled with occasional salty language. I write like a kid from Queens. And I don't always use the Queen's English.

Know that everything in each of my books is true. However, some names have been changed to keep me from being sued or punched in the face.

It is my sincere hope that after reading my books, you will take your own pen to paper and share your life and times with the people important to you. You don't need a plan. You don't need a goal. You don't even need an agent or a publisher. Just some time and a desire to share.

I believe that the greatest gift we have is not our collection of tchotchkes or other property. It is our stories. For who we are is the compilation of the stories of our lives. Although each story in this book is true and exactly as I was able to recall, I did take the liberty of changing some of the names. If you do recognize yourself in any of these stories, it is probably you. In which case I'm sorry. Or you're welcome.

Eric V. Litsky
Simsbury, CT

1

Pickles and Milhous Fly Again

What do you say to a guy in his underwear? Outside of his apartment. Holding an oversized bird cage with two chirping parakeets?

That guy was me. Here's what happened.

My college friend Jesse called and asked if he could stop by. My wife and I had just moved into an apartment in Great Neck. An affluent town on the North Shore of Long Island. I was excited to see him. I enjoyed his company immensely.

He wanted to ask us for a favor. And I hoped the visit was not to borrow money. We were close to broke and had none to spare. Although we finally had jobs. We were both underemployed.

Underemployed was a new word for me. It meant that your salary was not enough to cover your expenses. I was a liberal arts graduate. So what did I know?

We lived on the sixth floor of a building a few blocks from the railroad station. Every half hour the Long Island Railroad moved executives of all stripes and sizes to and from the city.

The year was 1973. I had just started my first real job. I was unhappy, depressed, and having difficulty finding emotional *terra firma* outside of the hallowed halls of academia.

We were struggling to keep our heads above water. Having already blown through whatever cash we received at our wedding. We were trying to figure out how to establish ourselves as newly minted college graduates. Wearing not yet paid off wedding rings.

We buzzed Jesse into the building. And waited for his knock.

And there was Jesse holding a very large birdcage. Containing two loudly chirping parakeets.

"Meet Pickles and Milhous. I've had them since graduation last year," he said, bursting with pride.

"Do you often walk around Great Neck with your bird in your hand?" I asked.

My wife shot me a dirty look for asking such a stupid question. Her dirty looks were the default position of our marriage. It might just be the reason that our new marriage was on borrowed time. Almost from the start.

"I need a small favor," he said. *"Can you sit for Pickles and Milhous this week? I'm going on vacation."*

For the record, I don't care much for animals. Especially those that belong outside hunting for worms. We had just gotten rid of my wife's awful cat.

She insisted on peeing in our bathtub. And shitting in my closet. The awful cat, that is. Not my wife. Though a couple of times the subject was open for debate.

Sitting across from us was a good friend who loved these little birds more than life itself. What else could I say?

"Sure, just tell us what to do," I said.

He explained how to place the newspaper on the bottom of the cage each morning. And fill the little cups attached to the inside of their little bird prison with water and seed.

With that, he gave their little peckers a kiss goodbye. And returned them to their cage. He'd be back in a week to retrieve them.

Before we could think better of our decision. He was out the door leaving us responsible for the care and well-being of his progeny.

A few days later I came home from work with a terrible headache. My wife would not be home for a while. I headed for the bedroom as Pickles and Milhous cheerfully tweeted away in our living room. Do birds ever tweet un-cheerfully?

I took off my pants. And laid down on the bed for a short nap. Sometime later I woke up to see red lights moving around on my bedroom ceiling.

At first, I thought I was still dreaming or perhaps in the middle of a UFO landing. Then I looked out the window and noticed the commotion six stories below.

Two fire trucks were unloading men and equipment. A few ran into our building with axes in hand. Shit! I smelled smoke.

"The fucking building is on fire!" I shouted to myself. I was awake enough to realize I had to get out of there fast. I quickly looked around at what to grab. But as newlyweds, we didn't own anything of much value.

I grabbed the birdcage and ran out.

Two things should have occurred to me before the door closed behind me.

First, our apartment door locked when the door closed. So we never left the apartment without a key. And second, my key was in my pants pocket.

Which was on the bed where I had been napping. Hence, no pants. And no keys.

So, there I was standing in the hallway in my underwear. Holding a bird cage with Pickles and Milhous happily chirping away.

"Nice birds – You forget something – Your wife's not home, is she? – Nice legs, by the way."

My neighbors smiled widely as they headed down the stairs to safety. Not one of them offered me a blanket or a pair of pants.

I just stood there for a few moments completely motionless. Unsure of what to do next.

"If I stay here," I thought, *"they might find me dead before too long."* It was a cold fall evening. The three of us were sure to freeze our peckers off if we went outside.

"Maybe I could run down the stairs to the super's office for a key. Or to borrow a pair of his pants."

These were the thoughts rolling through my head. The elevator door opened. Out stepped my wife. Along with a few of my neighbors. Still excited about running down six flights of stairs.

Turns out some kids set a mattress on fire in the alley. It was quickly extinguished.

My wife stared at me for a few moments. Unable to say anything. As she rummaged through her purse for her set of keys, she shook her head. Wondering if this was what the rest of her life would look like.

Pickles and Milhous looked at me too. I think they were smirking.

I never thought I'd miss my wife's awful cat. She would have wiped the smirks right off their little bird faces.

Jesse returned a few days later. Tanned, rested, and none the wiser.

2

Ass Doc

There I was with my ass in the air. Pants-less. Waiting for a proctologist to take a peek. At hopefully the *only* case of hemorrhoids I would ever have.

I cannot think of a time in my life when I felt more vulnerable.

Just as I thought this moment couldn't be any more embarrassing (pronounced in my head as em-bare-ass-ing) I heard footsteps in the hallway behind me. Yes. I said <u>behind</u>.

Someone had left the door ajar. And it was now fully open as I lay prone over a medical pommel horse. Listening to snippets of hallway conversation.

There was a little giggle here and there. I was certain that my exposed derriere was bringing joy to all who walked by.

I could feel my face blush, and wondered if butts blush too. Mine surely would have turned bright red.

My mind wandered as each minute felt like an hour buried up to my neck in a hill of red ants.

The last time I had been in this building it was the office of the real estate company for which I once worked. It was raided by the FBI and forced into bankruptcy. The principals ended up in Federal prison for the Ponzi scheme they had created.

Some years later the offices were totally gutted. Renovated into the medical space where my ass now hung out. For all the world to see.

I visualized where my current location would have been in the original office space. Only a few years earlier my ass would have been on full display in the middle of the large glass conference room. Hanging out there like a *jamon serrano* in a Madrid butcher shop. How fitting.

"Could this get any worse," I mumbled to myself.

*"Hi. I'm Dr. So and So. (*I recall that her name rhymed with rectum) *"Please don't get up,"* her attempt at a little humor as she walked in front of the pommel horse to talk to my face.

It had never occurred to me that this doctor would be a woman. I quickly glanced at her fingers. Delighted not to see long nails or sharp jewelry.

"Nice to meet you, too," I said with whatever charm I could muster.

"I have two interns on rotation with me. Would you mind if they joined in the exam," she asked.

"Sure. Let's make it a party." What else could I say?

I heard three sets of rubber gloves snap. That sound still makes me cringe. I don't know how long they poked and prodded around. Or for that matter who was doing the poking. And who was doing the prodding?

Finally, I was told to drink more water. And eat more salad. And I would be just fine.

Ten minutes and a $50 co-pay later I was in the empty elevator. Where I burst out in uncontainable laughter.

Who could I ever tell this story to?

3

— • —

THE CRAB APPLE TREE

My parents let me chop down the crab apple tree in our backyard. It was 25 feet tall. I was thirteen with a handheld hatchet. Begging the question:

What the hell were my parents thinking?

Each summer hundreds of crab apples would drop into our postage stamp-sized backyard. Where they mostly rotted in place.

We would throw them at each other. It was something like a snowball fight. Without the snow.

My brother Andy and I liked to climb to the top. We could peek over the roofline of our small brick cape and see the spire of the Empire State Building. Six miles and a world away.

But my parents were determined that the tree needed to come down. In order to bring a bit of sunshine to our small backyard. And to put an end to the annual convention of squirrels feasting on our rotting crab apples.

My parents got a couple of shockingly high estimates they couldn't afford. So, I stepped up and volunteered to take the tree down myself. I had been a Boy Scout for almost a year.

How hard could this be?

I had nothing much scheduled for my summer vacation. Andy was away for that summer. That left me solely in charge of doing stupid things.

I think my parents believed that giving me a project like this was a good way to keep me out of trouble. And out of their hair.

To be fair, my parents weren't idiots. Yet somehow, they simply did not grasp the danger of a thirteen-year-old swinging on branches 25 feet in the air. With a sharpened hatchet in hand.

I shimmied up the tree with my hatchet and started chopping. There was no rhyme or reason. I just knew I should not chop a branch while I was sitting on it. I learned that from years of cartoon watching.

Down the branches came. Filling our back yard. The lower ones were thicker. Some six inches in diameter.

After two weeks of chopping all that remained was a branchless tree. And I had a freakishly large right forearm that looked like it belonged to Popeye.

I was now left with a problem. How to get the tree down without doing damage to my house. Or taking out my neighbor's garage. Houses on my street were very close together.

I had not yet studied geometry. But I needed to determine the height of the tree.

I took a skein of yarn from my grandmother's knitting bag. My plan was to lasso the treetop and drop the yarn to the ground. That would give me the approximate height of the tree. I'd then stretch the yarn out to determine the best direction to drop the tree.

But first I needed something with some weight to attach to the end of my yarn so I could lasso the treetop.

The solution – my little sister Amy's doll. Her name was Betsy. She weighed about a pound.

I tied the yarn around Betsy's neck and threw her out of my parent's upstairs bedroom window. It took three tries to lasso the top of the tree.

I then ran back downstairs to find my sister freaking out.

"You killed Betsy," she said tearfully.

I looked up. Sure enough, there was Betsy. Hanging from her neck dangling 25 feet off the ground.

I might have promised my sister ice cream and a pony for her birthday to not rat me out to our parents. I still owe her the pony.

I yanked Betsy down from the tree. And returned her to my sister. A bit scuffed but no worse for wear.

I laid out the length of yarn. I figured I could drop the tree between a couple of backyard bushes. This is where the Boy Scouts should have taken away my merit badges.

I began chopping the tree in the direction of where I wanted it to fall. After some hours the tree started to creak. And then it fell. It bounced off my parent's garage. And hit the ground with a loud thud.

It landed precisely 50 feet from where I was aiming.

To be clear, our entire backyard was just 50 feet wide. So, you could say I dropped the tree *a yard* from where I was aiming. And I still had all of my appendages.

Not bad for a thirteen-year-old.

4

THE BELT

Much like Tom Sawyer's life took place along the Mississippi River, the events in my early life centered around a three-lane concrete highway called The Belt.

It was our connection to the world around us.

The highway runs from the Whitestone Bridge around the borough of Queens until it ends in Brooklyn. A little past JFK Airport.

Though maps and road signs identify this thoroughfare as The Cross Island Parkway, locals simply refer to it as The Belt.

On a map, it looks like a belt around a fat belly as it separates Queens from Nassau County on Long Island.

Or as they say on the Nassau side of the highway *Long Guyland*.

I'm a kid from Queens. More specifically, the working-class neighborhood of Cambria Heights, bordered on the east by The Belt Parkway. I suppose we had our own accents here, too. But to us, we *tawked normal*.

Back in those days, each neighborhood had a slight accent, virtually imperceptible to outsiders. But like a sommelier identifying the birthplace of a fine bottle of wine, some of us with a good ear could accurately tell who lived here.

Or in neighboring Laurelton to the south. Or Hollis to the north. These places are only a few minutes away in opposite directions along The Belt.

We lived four blocks from the Linden Blvd. exit. The overpass created a hill that ran down to the highway below.

Our community of Cambria Heights should have been called Cambria Flats. Nothing is elevated here. Except, that is, for the Linden Blvd. overpass.

The adjacent grassy slope was ominously named Dead Man's Hill. I don't know if a man ever died there but each winter a lot of us kids came dangerously close.

When we got a couple of inches of snow, my dad would throw our Flexible Flyers into the car. And drive my brother Andy and me up to Dead Man's Hill.

We would take turns with dozens of other youngsters careening down toward the oncoming highway traffic. At the last second, we would pull hard to the right on the wooden steering bar to keep from being run over by highway traffic. Back then there were no protective guard rails.

The most insane part of this was that so many of our dads stood at the top of the hill cheering their children's death-defying antics.

Perhaps it was that they survived the Great Depression. Or made it back in one piece from WWII. Or had too many kids at home and could afford to lose a few.

Even at age nine, I determined this was some really bad parenting. I promised myself I wouldn't intentionally try to kill any of my future children. I just barely kept that promise. But that is a story for another day.

Nevertheless, sledding so close to death was a crapload of fun. No one gave safety much thought.

On summer days we'd ride our bikes across the Linden Blvd. overpass to Carvel Ice Cream. A few short blocks into *enemy territory*. This was more dangerous to us than speeding down an icy-covered Dead Man's Hill.

This is where we'd often see the boys from Elmont. The other side of The Belt was Elmont. It was outside the city limits in a strange and often dangerous land called Long Island.

A couple of times we got chased back over the highway to the safety of our neighborhood. By bigger boys with faster bikes.

"Get back on your side of The Belt!" they would shout feigning a frontal assault.

"We better not ever see you here again or you know what's gonna happen," they threatened.

No, we had no idea what *gonna happen* meant. Only that it wouldn't be good. And they were bigger than us. And a few years older.

But that didn't stop us. We screwed up our courage and rode over anyway. The taste of a soft serve Carvel cone on a hot summer day was a risk worth taking. The only real challenge was consuming it before it melted all over us and our bikes in the hot sun.

Belmont Racetrack was only a few minutes further by bike from Linden Blvd. We discovered an opening in the fence in the southernmost parking lot. We didn't know or care about horse racing or the racetrack. What drew us here was a gigantic asphalt parking lot.

On non-race days several of us would ride up along the service road of The Belt to our *secret* entrance and sneak into Belmont's parking lot. It was huge.

We'd carry broomsticks and several Spaulding Pinkie rubber balls. And have the best stickball games ever. Unimpeded by traffic, parked cars, tree branches, and the occasional broken window back on 233rd St.

Also close to my home, The Belt divides. The highway forks to create the Southern State Parkway. That takes you to the first of Long Island's nouveau riche cluster of suburbs called the Five Towns. But we rarely ventured there. Kids from Queens were not welcome.

The Belt then continues toward JFK and Brooklyn.

At that forked intersection, there is a patch of grass bordered by the two highways and their entrance ramps. This is where we played tackle football.

We all played with helmets. I bought mine, a $12 plastic helmet, at the Green Acres Shopping Center a few minutes further down The Belt. I had a newspaper route back then and always kept some cash hidden in my sock drawer for such emergency purchases.

A few of the kids had shoulder pads. I was a baseball catcher so at least I had a cup enabling me to have a family someday.

There were some scrapes and bruises. But surprisingly, not much blood. The football rarely found its way into the traffic on The Belt.

More dangerous than highway traffic was getting crushed by a few opposing players who actually knew how to play football. They were well-padded and hit hard.

A block or two from our make-shift football field was a city-operated baseball field. By early high school, many of us could launch home runs over the fifteen-foot-high centerfield fence into the traffic on The Belt.

Whenever I'd hit one over, I would pause running to first base. Watch the ball clear the fence. And wait a moment for the sound of a screech or crash on the highway. Hearing nothing, I would continue my trot around the bases.

Living along The Belt wasn't all sports. I was a Cub Scout when I was young. Our Scout Master once took us on an outing into the woods to learn about nature.

We went to Crocheron Park a forty-acre wooded green space set back off The Belt. Though it wasn't the Adirondacks or The Catskills, it was the largest wooded area close to home. A ten-minute drive on The Belt to the Bayside exit. And *voilà!* We were deep in the only woods we knew.

At the age of eight, I was a combination of Daniel Boone and Davy Crocket (both TV shows of the day) combing the woods for wild animals and men of ill will to throttle. My scouting days did not last long.

In my teenage years, The Belt Parkway also served as an outlet of laughter.

My brother Andy once took out a wooden light pole in the 1956 indestructible Plymouth we shared in high school. The pole rather spectacularly fell to the ground. The Plymouth was driven away, dented but proud.

When Belmont Racetrack let out on a Saturday afternoon, my friends and I occasionally found ourselves at a standstill on The Belt. Invariably someone would yell – *Chinese Fire Drill!*

With that, the four doors swung open. And we all ran around the car two or three times. Much to the delight of everyone else stuck in the same highway traffic jam.

On an otherwise quiet Saturday night, we would hop on The Belt and drive 10 minutes to JFK Airport. These were the days before any serious security. We'd park our car at either the TWA or PAN AM terminal and walk in. Right up to the gate.

We'd welcome travelers back home. Or wish them a hearty *Bon Voyage*. Leading us to wonder what life might be like wherever they were headed.

There was always lots of laughter there especially when we tried on foreign accents. Or attempted to flirt with girls. Occasionally, we'd get too rowdy, and we'd get thrown out.

To me, The Belt was much more than a highway. It took us and our imaginations to a world far outside our little corner of Queens. A corner I loved. But I could not get away from it fast enough.

5

— • —

Hanging Paper

H issing steam. Razor blades. Glue. And graffiti. Now that's what a nine-year-old calls a fun time.

Wallpaper adorning one's home in the 1950s sent a message to all who entered. That you were sophisticated. Stylish. And affluent. And who didn't want to be all of that?

Of course, this included my parents in our 1,250 sq. ft. cape-styled, brick home.

After chatting with the ladies of the PTA, my mother decided that it was time to make an upgrade in the look of our little home.

"I'm going to dreckorate the dinette," she said with a mix of determination and pride.

The translation of the word *dreck* is from Yiddish. It means *shit*. Or worthless crap.

I believe the term *dreckorating* was first used by my great-grandmother, Ida. The first of our family to set foot on American soil at the turn of the last century. She had no patience for silly, non-utilitarian decorations. To her it was all *dreck*. Thus *dreckorating*.

But this is the expression my mother used when she wanted to improve the aesthetics of our home. The term *dreckorating* was always accompanied with a smile.

We had no formal dining room. Homework was done. Board games were played. Our meals were eaten on the table in the half-sized room attached to the kitchen called the dinette.

It was the heartbeat of our family home.

And so, it was my mother's mission to re-wallpaper our dinette.

Now there is no place on earth more boring for a nine-year-old and an eleven-year-old than to be stuck in a store full of wallpaper on a beautiful afternoon.

My brother and I annoyed my mother so much in the store that she bribed us to shut up. And sit quietly as she picked through endless wall-covering choices.

"When we get home you guys can write on the walls of the dinette. We'll be covering them anyway."

That magic incantation carried us through the agonizing ordeal.

After what seemed like a lifetime, my mother finally picked out a pattern. We walked out of the store with us helping her carry a half dozen rolls of wallpaper. Along with glue, brushes, razor blades, a stepstool, and a yardstick.

The previous week had been spent with her and my dad steaming the old wallpaper off the dinette walls. Each night they would fill a vacuum-sized contraption with water. Plug it into the wall. And put the steam-hissing applicator directly onto the wallpaper.

It would eventually loosen the glue. So that the pieces of soggy wallpaper would finally release its grip. And drop to the floor.

Andy and I heard some new words as the hissing steam burned their forearms. My mother shouted them in Yiddish. My father repeatedly shouted, *"Jesus H. Christ!"* which confused me on many levels.

First, we were Jewish. So I didn't know how Jesus ended up in our dinette.

And second, I remembered hearing The Lord's Prayer from some Catholic friends once. I heard the first line as *"Our Father who art in heaven, Harold be thy name."*

My father's name was Harold. Maybe Harold was Jesus' middle name. It was a puzzle.

Night after night they cursed the walls of our small dinette. Until the last shred of paper surrendered and fell.

My mother's plan was to paper the walls by herself.

How hard could that be?

My mother stayed home raising the four of us. Though she spent much of her time connected to the wall phone that hung in our kitchen. Rather than providing us with much, if any, structure or guidance.

We were largely left unsupervised. Free to explore the world around us. Expressing ourselves however we chose.

Upon our return from the wallpaper store, Andy and I shot out of the station wagon. Barely waiting for the car to come to a complete stop. We couldn't get our markers, pens and crayons out fast enough.

We spent the next hour engaged in the art of graffiti. Writing, drawing and cartooning all over the soon to be covered walls of our dinette.

Mrs. Nagle (my third-grade teacher) *is a big fat ass-face.* This was accompanied by an equally inappropriate drawing.... more or less anatomically correct.

We wrote the words **Shit**, **Fart** and **Puke** any number of times. Although I think I misspelled puke. It became puck.

PS 176 rules. Zorro (Andy's hero). **Superman** (my hero). Along with a dozen games of tic tac toe and hangman.

To our amazement my parents didn't seem to care that the room was covered in our elementary school graffiti.

The new wallpaper pattern was simple. It took my mother a day to paste it up and trim. Just in time for her to entertain the ladies of the PTA who came for coffee and gossip a few days later.

The coffee was poured. The Entenmann's coffee cake was served. Edith, Irma and Zelda settled in for a nice afternoon chat.

"Betty, what is that on the walls?" asked Edith, as she looked over the top of her glasses.

"My new wallpaper. I did it myself," my mom said as she turned around to see that our elementary school graffiti was ever so slowly bleeding through the paper.

My mother was absolutely horrified as her friends giggled.

I am told that Zelda particularly liked my drawing of Mrs. Nagle, my ass-faced 3rd grade teacher. Irma wanted to know why we wrote the word Puck. Or if the P was really an unusually formed F.

There was laughter and, of course, some embarrassment.

But Andy and I were in the clear. And this was the last time either of us ever wrote on the walls of our home. Or for that matter, ever wallpapered.

6

THE DAY OF THE WATER WARS

I suppose I'd have to blame it on the Greenbergs. They weren't home when Joey and I knocked on the door to see if one of the Greenberg boys wanted to come out and play.

It was an early summer weekend day. Perhaps they were off to Jones Beach or to a family gathering.

As we stepped off the porch, I noticed a crate of seltzer. The Greenbergs got a seltzer delivery every week. But this was the first time I noticed this treasure of fun. Twelve bottles with squirters on top begging for us to depress.

Seltzer is simply carbonated water. The water is compressed in these bottles giving it a shooting range of about six-feet. They are common in bars for mixed drinks. But in the hands of a circus clown. Or a couple of young teenagers. It is 100% pure fun.

What else could we do?

I bent down and pulled a bottle out of the wooden crate. Without warning I gave Joey a quick squirt dead square in the center of his chest.

He feigned he was shot and then quickly retaliated. The battle ensued. A few minutes later we were soaked. And screaming with laughter.

We emptied four of their twelve bottles. I'm sure we had more fun with them than the Greenbergs ever would.

We put the used bottles back in the crate. And hoped that the water on the wet driveway would evaporate quickly on that warm July day.

We walked back down 233rd St. to my house. To find my mother standing with arms crossed at our front door. She was really annoyed at my tardiness. I was supposed to have been home an hour earlier. She never noticed or asked why we were both soaking wet.

She needed to *do the marketing,* her words for going to the Grand Union to buy food. To me, it sounded like something you would say in a Madison Avenue ad agency.

"Stay with your brother and I'll be back in an hour or so," she said as she maneuvered the oversized family station wagon out of our undersized driveway.

The ten-year-old Chevy station wagon could seat our whole family. All six of us. That is so long as one or two of us crawled in the *way back,* (our term for the third row of backward seating) that left our noses pressed perilously close to the rear window.

But this is not what made the car a death trap. This old thing had significant rust. The floor in the front passenger side had completely disintegrated.

If you pulled up the thin carpet and the metal dish pan my dad placed over it as an attempted repair, you could see the road pass by below. We called this car our Fred Flintstone car.

The front passenger seat was normally referred to simply as *shotgun,* a homage to the wagon train riders of the Wild West. The guy to the right of the driver carried a shotgun for protection from robbers. Our shotgun seat was called, "*Yabba dabba do!*" A tip of the hat to Mr. Flintstone.

As soon as my mother pulled out of the driveway my little brother Tom said, "*Let's play war.*"

He pulled out his water gun and gave me a squirt. Joey and I found water pistols of our own. And the battle quickly escalated as wars generally do. On came the water balloons. And then water by the bucket.

What ended our war was not a negotiated truce. Or unconditional surrender. It was my mother coming home from the grocery store.

She caught me spraying Tom with a garden hose through his first-floor bedroom window.

Caught me dead to rights! I thought about telling her that Tom was playing with matches. And I was saving our home. But he was only five. And I was clearly busted.

I was grounded for a week. My father reduced my sentence to a few days confined to my room. At least I had my transistor radio and the Playboy Magazine I had stolen from my cousin Jeff.

War is hell.

7

WITH SIX YOU GET EGGROLL

Even though my brother Tom was an infant with no teeth, we still were a family of six. And qualified for free eggrolls.

I was ten when I first saw the bright red neon sign on Merrick Blvd.

With Six You Get Eggroll. Inviting families for an inexpensive meal. Plus a round of free eggrolls.

The House of Chang was my first experience with Asian food. More accurately it was Chinese food. Or at least what Americans in 1961 thought was Chinese food.

These were the days of Chairman Mao. And a billion near-starving Chinese people our government refused to recognize. A half century later the world changed. So did our taste buds.

It was a big deal when our family went out for dinner. There was nothing better than trading off the meat and potatoes my mother would burn. For the exotic tastes from the Far East.

Tastes like chicken chow mein, spareribs, pork fried rice, and the delightful won ton soup. I get hungry just writing this.

There is a tradition of Jews in America eating Chinese food on Sundays. I imagine it started in my grandparents' generation in the melting pot of immigrants on the Lower East Side of NY.

I'm pretty sure my grandparents didn't call out for Chinese from their shtetl (ghetto) in Eastern Europe at the turn of the last century.

Much like Jewish cuisine, Chinese food has a history of being a diverse and adaptable cuisine. Chinese restaurants were generally open on Sundays when other restaurants were not.

This made for a perfect time to splurge a little. And take the family out at the end of a long week.

We were taken to a booth with a white tablecloth. Set with white porcelain plates trimmed with a pencil-thin red stripe. In addition to a fork and spoon, each setting had chopsticks. Which none of us knew how to use.

My brother Andy and I always dueled with the chopsticks. Until my father took them away.

A large bowl of crispy noodles came with several smaller bowls of sweet duck sauce and spicy mustard for the dipping.

I went for the staple. Tried and true chicken chow mein. Andy had more adventurous tastes. He talked my father into spending an extra dollar on shrimp and lobster sauce with a side of pork fried rice.

My five-year-old sister Amy only wanted rice. Boring white rice. And more crispy noodles to dip. My parents shared a dish of steak with pepper sauce. It gave my mother indigestion. A fair turn of events, since it was her cooking that usually gave us indigestion.

We also had Chinese tea in little cups that fit perfectly into our hands. Four teaspoons of sugar made it very, very tasty. Never too early to get our bodies primed for diabetes.

It didn't take long before our white tablecloth was covered in multi-colored drippings. From the sauces and mustards. What a glorious mess we made.

We lived in a working-class neighborhood. My dad supported our family of six on a cop's salary. But there was always a little extra in an otherwise tight budget, to take the family out for Chinese on a Sunday.

The grand finale was the fortune cookies. Marking the end of a satisfying and scrumptious meal. We read each paper fortune as though they were dialogue from a Charlie Chan movie. It was funny as hell. In the 1960's there was no such thing as being politically correct.

As the years passed my taste in Chinese fare widened, including unique tastes from provinces of Hunan, Szechuan, Mandarin, Canton, and others.

In my college years, I found that a Chinese dinner was an affordable date. The best value for a broke college student was the pupu platter.

Pupu platters are a cardiologist's worst nightmare. A platter teeming with deep-fried, artery-clogging appetizers. Including chicken, shrimp, and a vegetable or two. As well as the very un-Chinese fried mozzarella sticks.

All this was accompanied by a large array of dipping sauces. Ranging in spiciness from sweet to *holy-shit-that's-hot!*

At the center of the platter is a flame. The idea is to spear your already fried appetizer with a thin stick they provide. Then you hold it over the flame for that extra crispy taste. Before finally dipping it in your choice of sauces.

On one memorable evening my stick caught on fire. When I leaned down to blow it out my shoulder length hair joined in the party. A conflagration! Yes, my hair caught fire in a crowded Chinese restaurant on a Sunday night.

In one motion I put my cupped hands in the water pitcher. As I leapt up expressing myself with a string of inappropriate exclamations. And tamped out the fire on top of my head.

Burnt hair is a smell not easily ignored. Nor easily forgotten. The restaurant emptied quickly. My date was horrified. As nonplussed as I could be, I grabbed a new stick. Then sat back and finished my pupu platter.

To this day, each time I see it offered as an appetizer on a menu I remember the smell of burnt hair. Mine.

I have not ordered one since.

Today, my wife Norma and I regularly eat a wide variety of Asian cuisine. Japanese. Thai. Vietnamese. Korean. Even Mongolian.

But none of it comes to the table on fire.

8

HEROES

I jumped off the top of a building. And flew down to a railroad track where a pretty girl from my first-grade class was tied up. A freight train was speeding toward us. Smoke billowing from the locomotive. I had just a moment to untie her. And fly her back to safety.

Mighty Mouse was there, too. His theme song was playing. A crowd gathered and cheered. We were all as happy as could be.

This is the earliest dream I can remember. I was six. And clearly had a need to perform an act of heroism. Perhaps that was the result of watching too many cartoons. Superman episodes. Or war movies.

It is said that a hero is someone who provides exceptional courage or bravery in the face of adversity or challenging circumstances.

But in my personal experience, a hero is usually ignored. Laughed at. And sometimes shit upon.

Here are three personal examples from my life.

I worked as a waiter in a resort the summer before entering college. I had just put eight lunches on the table. And was delighted that I did it without spilling anything. Or leaving my thumbprint in any of the food. I was a lousy waiter.

A moment later a middle-aged man at my table grabbed his chest and fell to the floor. His wife let out a scream. An otherwise noisy dining room fell deadly silent. I felt all eyes on me. As I was standing over the guy on the floor.

I had some training as a lifeguard. So I knew rudimentary CPR. I didn't see anyone else moving toward him. I did a quick assessment. He was not breathing. I checked his mouth to make sure there were no obstructions.

Just then, one of the busboys joined me. He had been an Eagle Scout and knew more than me. He started chest compressions as I tried to breathe life into the now still body.

As you can imagine a lot went through my mind. I'm not a religious man. But in my eighteen years I had never prayed so hard for a miracle.

There I was with my lips on another man's mouth. In front of a room full of people expecting to witness a positive outcome.

The rule with CPR is that you don't quit until trained medical people arrive and take charge. We went for about twenty minutes.... the longest twenty minutes of my life. Finally, a local doctor came in and pronounced him dead.

I'm guessing that he was dead before he hit the floor. But I never asked for confirmation.

The dining room cleared out. The coroner arrived and took the body away a short time later. He took down our names and asked a few questions. Then I went back to the bunkhouse.

I rinsed my mouth out with some bourbon one of the guys had. And I proceeded to take a nap to quiet down the adrenalin that had been surging through my body for the past hour.

Three hours later we were setting up for the dinner meal as if nothing had happened. No one spoke of the incident. No one asked if I was OK. I had the feeling that people looked at me as though I let everyone down. That I let the guy die.

I was completely ignored. And I didn't speak of this again until this writing. My family never knew of this incident.

Twenty-five years later, my lifeguard experience would once again be called into action. This time it resulted in a boatload of laughter.

I was with some friends on a houseboat on Lake Powell. Engaged in a personal growth workshop. Most of us knew one another from previous programs.

There was a strong feeling of camaraderie as we experienced the beauty of this amazing place. In the middle of a lake. In the middle of a desert. Somewhere in Utah.

Lake Powell was created by artificially damming up the Colorado River at Glen Canyon. The river then flows toward the Grand Canyon a hundred miles away. Lake Powell is some 250 miles long with depths reaching 500 feet or more.

These deep blue waters are dramatically contrasted with the muted orange and red clay earth tones of the surrounding desert. The land has all the feel of the lunar surface. As far as the eye can see there are inlets and ranges of buttes and plateaus rising from what were once the tops of canyon walls.

While underway our houseboat could legally carry only 15 passengers. There were 20 of us. So, in order to comply with the National Park Service rules, we took turns riding in the 14 ft. motorboat which trailed along behind.

Surrounded by such mesmerizing beauty we got a little lackadaisical with our safety.

I noticed food being thrown to those on the motorboat. As it bounced through the wake of the houseboat. In a split second, there was a terrible grinding sound. The little motorboat was pulled under the houseboat, unable to repel from its wake. Leaving five of our friends in very deep water.

Instinct kicked in.

I ran toward the rear of the boat kicking off my sandals. And dropping my pants on the deck. I kept my eyes on the five people in the water the entire time.

Without thinking, I leaped over the railing. And did a perfect lifeguard dive – legs spread front to back. Arms spread side to side. So, my head would not go under the water and lose sight of the swimmers.

Of course, I never considered that I was flying through the air in nothing by my *whitey tighties.*

A few moments later I got to their dinghy. I found my five friends were all safe. Laughing hysterically at the sight of me flying off the houseboat in my underpants. That moment of comic relief did help to calm everyone's nerves.

But I don't believe they teach that in Red Cross Lifeguard school.

We quickly flipped the little boat back over and continued our wonderful week. This time, more mindful of safety.

It was a beautiful spring afternoon. The sun was brightly shining. Temperature in the mid-70's. I had worked in the yard for a couple of hours. And now I was going to crack open the new Daniel Silva novel. And enjoy some *me time*. On my favorite lounge chair in my front yard.

There was a hummingbird hovering over the annuals I had just planted. I had an iced tea and a small bag of chips to nosh on. I love reading in the sunshine.

It was a perfect day. A few puffy clouds. Clear skies.

A couple of pages into my new book I noticed a young girl taking her small dog for a walk.

How lovely, I thought to myself.

As she approached my house, I noticed that my neighbor's two large standard poodles were loose. They were looking to make this little dog their afternoon snack.

The little girl screamed. All three dogs were barking loudly. And the poodles were about ready to pounce.

I don't know anything about dogs. Or little girls for that matter. I dropped my book and ran over. I picked up the little dog and turned to the poodles.

"Back the fuck off!" I shouted at them in my loudest and angriest voice. And, to my surprise and delight, they backed off.

I carried the little dog. Holding the little girl's hand we walked back up the street toward her house. In that moment I felt heroic. A combination of John Wayne. Superman or maybe Mighty Mouse who would utter, *"Here I come to save the day!"* And then did.

And then I smelled it. The poodles had literally scared the shit out of that little dog. And now the shit was all over me.

A lot went through my head as I walked back home.

I passed another neighbor out for a walk. She smiled and waved walking closer to engage me in conversation. Until she got within smelling distance. I could see she was having trouble understanding why I had shit all over me.

She gave me a quizzical look. I simply waved and kept walking. Neither wanting to explain nor extend my time in these awful-smelling clothes.

Walking home I thought about heroism. And the qualities that make a hero. I don't think it is limited to someone who slays the metaphorical dragon. Or rescues the damsel in distress.

I think heroism has more to do with raising a family. Working hard. Being honest. Being a good neighbor. A good citizen. Just trying to *do the right thing.*

We live in a world of unsung heroes. Our teachers. Our merchants. The postman. Our neighbors. They are everywhere. Perhaps we should sing their praises a little louder. And a little more often.

9

— • —

PUMPING IRON

My father loved to be in uniform. From my earliest years, he would regale us with how important it was to be a team member. The key to being on that team was to be in uniform.

"When everyone is dressed the same, no one cares where you came from. You are an equal part of the team," he would say.

As a teenager, a few years before World War II, he left his home on the Lower East Side of Manhattan and entered the US Merchant Marine Academy. It was there he donned a uniform for the first time.

When the war broke out, he put on Navy whites. A first lieutenant, second in command of a destroyer.

After the war, he enrolled in the Police Academy. He then proudly wore his NYPD blue uniform each day of his working life.

It was in that spirit that I was full of pride upon receiving my very first uniform. I was a member of the Cambria Heights Pirates. Number 18. Sponsored by A to Z Hardware.

I was eight years old. And I was an official Little Leaguer.

The uniform came in a clear plastic bag. It included pants, a button-down shirt, a pair of blue-striped stirrup socks along with my very own baseball cap. My little heart was bursting out of my chest. I was a part of my first team ever.

The only issue was I had no idea how to play baseball. In fact, I had never even played catch. My dad had bursitis which always sounded to me like a made-up word. So, he couldn't throw a ball. And my older brother Andy had no real interest in the game.

Besides we only had just one baseball glove between us. My parents made us share it.

The old leather glove had been kicking around my family since DiMaggio was in diapers. It was two inches thick and looked more like second base than a baseball glove. Also, it was too big for my little hand. Even if I were lucky enough to catch a ball, I wouldn't be able to squeeze the glove to hold it.

I recently saw a glove just like it at the Baseball Hall of Fame. I think that one belonged to Ty Cobb. Or some other dead guy who'd been in the Hall since the 1930s.

Sometime after the first practice, Andy found that he was actually left-handed. So, he got a new glove. I didn't mind. I now had a glove of my very own.

The Cambria Heights Pirates were comprised of neighborhood kids ten and eleven years old. They were two or three years older than me. My parents might have lied about my age so Andy and I could be on the same team.

Driving us to different fields at different times was not going to work for my family. My mother didn't start driving until later. And my father worked unpredictable hours. Sometimes sleeping all day after working an all-night shift. It was weird growing up being the son of a cop.

After several practices during which I neither caught nor came close to hitting a baseball, the season began.

We were scheduled to play the Cambria Heights Yankees on Saturday. They were sponsored by Sullivan's Insurance. We'd get a calendar and birthday cards from them every year.

We were sponsored by A to Z, a hardware/variety store that sold everything from A to Z. From time to time I wondered what they sold beginning with the letter Z. Or for that matter X.

Meanwhile, I could hardly contain myself waiting for Saturday. This was so exciting. My first game on my first team.

I remembered what my dad taught me about uniforms. And how important it was to have them crisp.

That morning I woke up early and took out the ironing board which luckily opened exactly to the height of my waist. About two feet off the floor.

Next, I took out the iron and plugged it in. I didn't know what the settings were for. So, I just dialed the knob as far as it would go. I figured it needed to be hot.

And hot it was.

I remembered watching my grandmother iron. And how she put a crease in my grandfather's pants. This was harder than it looked. But I persevered. Although I burned my hand several times, I did a pretty good job making creases in my baseball uniform pants.

When I was finished, I ran to show my parents what I had done. In my excitement I inadvertently tripped over the chord unplugging the iron. Otherwise, it might have remained on all day. And that would not be the last time I nearly burned down my house.

We got to the Little League field right on time for the start of the noon game. I noticed that I was the only player who had a crease in his uniform pants and a neatly ironed uniform shirt. I felt so proud.

The Cambria Heights Pirates took the field. Andy and I remained in the dugout sitting on the bench.

The Little League rules said every player needed to get on the field for an inning and get at least one at-bat in each game. I knew my time would come.

Meanwhile, I sat on the bench with my hand in my glove so as not to show the burn marks on my thumb and index finger.

Our star player, Tommy, came up in the fifth inning. He mimicked the major league batters he had seen on TV. He tapped his sneakers to knock the mud out of his cleats. But there was no mud. And he wasn't wearing cleats. They were Keds.

He smacked the inside of his ankle bone. And went down like a shot. He cried like a baby.

Decades later, I thought back to my first game after hearing Tom Hanks yell out, *"There's no crying in baseball,"* from the wonderful movie *A League of Their Own.*

Tom.... I gotta tell you. Sometimes there is!

"Eric. Grab a bat and a helmet. You're pinch-hitting for Tommy," Coach Walker shouted. That guy was always shouting.

"A walk is as good as a hit," someone yelled.

"Let's go batter, batter, batter," another chimed in.

At first, I was terrified stepping up to the plate in my crisply ironed uniform. But I was a part of this team. I belonged. And I was damn well going to do my best.

I was a head shorter than everyone else on my team. My hands were positioned backward on the bat. Had I swung hard I might have broken my skinny wrist. But I never got to swing the bat.

The first pitch hit me square in the ass as I turned away from it. As I trotted down to first base everyone cheered.

Why are they cheering me? I thought. *All I did was get hit in the ass with the baseball.*

It would be years before I would hear cheers from actually doing something on the field.

My first season ended with my never hitting or catching a baseball. But I showed up each week wearing a crisply ironed uniform. With fewer and fewer burns on my hands.

10

HE DID WHAT?

And then the Rabbi farted.

But that is the end of the story. Let's start somewhere near the beginning.

It was October 1960. Chubby Checker had the number-one record in the country. The Twist. We still dance to it.

Alfred Hitchcock's *Psycho* packed movie theaters. I often think of that shower scene when I lather up.

And there was some talk of President Eisenhower sending 3,500 peace-keeping troops to a place no one had ever heard of – Vietnam.

Kennedy and Nixon battled to become the leader of the free world. Kennedy would win but he would not finish his first term. Nixon would make a comeback eight years later. Only to resign in disgrace.

But the big talk in October of 1960 in New York was the World Series. The powerhouse NY Yankees vs. the Pittsburg Pirates. And the winner of the best of seven series would decide who indeed was the best in the land.

Meanwhile, I was a nine-year-old just discovering baseball. Both the Brooklyn Dodgers *and* the NY Giants had taken off to California a few years earlier.

The Yankees became the dominant sports team in NY. And probably the rest of the world as well. I was hooked. So were my friends. We loved the Yankees.

This was the year I started Hebrew school. In hopes that in four short years I'd learn enough Hebrew to get through my Bar Mitzvah. That seemed a lifetime away. Particularly since I could barely read English. Let alone that squiggly concoction of letters called Hebrew.

Off to the synagogue I went. Each Wednesday after school. And every Saturday morning. A bunch of us usually walked over together. After first filling our pockets at Adaline's Candy Store.

Our synagogue was Temple Torah. It was located in an empty storefront previously home to a small hardware store. About a mile from my house.

This was a small congregation, maybe forty families. Our observance of Judaism was Reform – simple translation *more English, less Hebrew.* As opposed to the more conservative religious observances of our kosher grandparents – *all Hebrew, no English.*

"This is not 19th century Russia. It is 1960. We don't live in a shtetl. It's a new decade in a fast-changing world. We are reform Jews," my non-Hebrew-reading father would say.

Temple Torah didn't have much money. The men in the congregation had partitioned off a few classrooms. And installed a couple of bathrooms. The remaining interior space was the sanctuary where we'd hold services.

There were no cushioned pews here. Just a bunch of uncomfortable metal folding chairs we'd take turns setting up each week.

At the front of the sanctuary, there was a raised platform. That's where the Rabbi conducted services.

Behind him was the ark. A decorated cabinet that held our Torah. The sacred text of our people. The Torah is the handwritten scroll of the first five books of the Old Testament.

Wealthier congregations have several Torahs in their arks in highly adorned and ornamented cases. We had just one.

Our religion teacher was the mother of one of my friends. She was a convert who grew up a Baptist in the South. But she knew the Old Testament better than any Rabbi we'd ever known.

Our small congregation couldn't afford to pay for a full-time Rabbi. So we hired a rotating crop of rabbinical students.

They were young and idealistic. Sometimes the Rabbi would be either a beatnik or a socialist. This often led to loud disagreements. And my people excel at verbal fisticuffs.

But a rotation of student rabbis was all we could afford.

Except in 1960. That was the year we hired Rabbi Mendel Guttman. He came out of retirement for this gig. To us, he was 100 years old. In retrospect, he was probably in his late 60s. He hunched over a bit. And had a short, scraggly gray beard.

He was from a strange and foreign land. Pittsburgh. Moreover, he was, of all things, an unapologetic Pittsburgh Pirates fan.

The World Series began the week after the Jewish New Year. Pirates vs. Yankees. Game on!

The first game was on a Wednesday afternoon. Almost all of the boys at Hebrew School that day, and each game day thereafter, hid small transistor radios in their shirt pockets. With earpieces so as not to be completely obvious.

The World Series games were day games in those days. The first game ended about 3:30 PM, just as the Hebrew classes began.

I saw Rabbi Guttman. He was doing a little jig in the hallway trying hard not to be noticed. He had his own earpiece in and wore a huge smile on his face. Pittsburgh won the first game 6-4.

It was at that moment I decided I liked this guy. Even though he was a Pirates fan.

Over the next week, the Series games went back and forth. Finally, both teams were deadlocked. Three games each. All would be decided in the final seventh game. It was all very exciting.

The lead in the seventh game changed hands several times until the bottom of the ninth inning. They were tied 9-9.

Then up came the Pirates.

And with one swing of the bat, Bill Mazeroski smashed a historic home run over the left field wall. Winning the game and crowning the Pirates as World Series Champions.

We were crushed as our stunned New York Yankees shuffled back into the dugout. The now second-best team in the game.

But baseball is not why you kept reading this story. You wanted to read about the Rabbi farting.

At the Friday night service that week, Rabbi Guttman was the only happy man in the synagogue. He was on top of the world as his Pirates defeated a much better team to become World Series Champions.

As he silently read a particularly solemn prayer a small toot was heard. Since the congregation was in quiet meditation, the sound echoed through the sanctuary.

The adults hushed the giggling children hoping that the toot was simply the sound of one of the rubber caps from a folding chair scraping on the vinyl floor. It was not.

A few moments later there would be no doubt. The Rabbi was unable to muffle the sound of his second fart under his flowing white robe. The sound that emanated was wildly out of place in this sacred space.

The lectern from where he spoke had an open mike. Amplifying the sound of his fart as it echoed through the room.

When he finished his passage – both the prayer *and* the fart – he paused and surveyed his congregants in silence. A hundred thoughts must have passed through his mind. But there just was nothing to be said.

He simply smiled. Briefly nodded his head. And continued with the service. As though farting in a synagogue was perfectly natural.

From time to time I think about that week back in October of 1960. When both the Pittsburgh Pirates and Rabbi Mendel Guttman came from behind.

11

— • —

Unprepared and Snowbound

A snowstorm snafu. Parents left high and dry. And a baby... you get the picture.

It was a crisp and clear Saturday afternoon a couple of weeks after the ball dropped in Times Square ringing in 1967.

My parents had invited some neighborhood friends over for a mid-day nosh. That's Jewish for coffee and rugelach. Sweet round pieces of culinary heaven. Each one about the size of a Dunkin Donuts donut hole. But trust me – way better.

My mother wanted a few friends to come by to meet her favorite nephew, Richard. He was coming over with his wife and new baby. She loved to show off her family to friends.

Richard is my first cousin. Ten years older.

I liked him. He was a little on the wild side. The first in my family to own a motorcycle. A new wife and baby had settled him down.

He owned his own yellow cab which was a big deal in those days. A NYC taxi medallion back then cost about as much as a single-family house in a nice part of Queens.

My brother Andy and I also had some friends over to play poker in our basement. Nickel, dime, quarter. Five card draw. Seven card stud. And of course, baseball. Where sixes and threes were wild. Maybe nines, too. The rules changed depending on who was dealing. And who could get away with what.

The buy-in was about $10. None of us had much money. Mostly we smoked. Swapped funny stories. And gossiped about the high school girls whose bra sizes made an impression on us.

On a good day, you could win $5-10. Richard asked to sit in. He did. And he did not have a good day. Over the course of an hour his wallet emptied. It was nice of him to provide us with beer and cigarette money for the next month.

He trudged back upstairs. Broke and dejected. I felt badly. But not enough to give him his money back.

Our friends left just as it started to snow. Creating a pretty scene that late Sunday afternoon. We rarely got much snow.

My parents' friends also headed out. My mother put some sandwiches together as the baby went down for a nap.

And the snow kept falling.

A while later, we discovered that this was no ordinary snowfall. It was really piling up. Several inches per hour.

Before we knew it there was a foot of snow with accompanying drifts two or three times higher. Richard and family weren't going anywhere.

This was a blizzard. And no one saw it coming.

The city of New York was completely unprepared. It would take days before the streets were finally cleared. You could barely make out the shape of Richard's taxi parked in front of our house.

Richard and family would need to spend the night – maybe longer.

But first, we had to solve two problems. The baby had only one diaper left. And other than rugelach there wasn't much else to eat.

I volunteered to trudge over to Jim's, a family-run bodega, three blocks away.

By the time I got there, his shelves were mostly bare. It looked like photos I'd seen of stores behind the Iron Curtain.

I grabbed the last box of newborn diapers. A few cans of soup. And some cold cuts and bread. It took a half hour to slog home back down the unplowed street. I finally arrived frozen and soaked from my waist to my sopping sneakers.

Meanwhile, my mother found two boxes of spaghetti. But we had no sauce. She sent my sister Amy next door to borrow a couple of cans of tomatoes from Gertie and George. They always had a full pantry. They were Italian. Of course, they would have cans of tomatoes.

Now my mother was not much of a cook. The only spices she owned were salt, pepper, and paprika. She assumed you opened the cans of tomatoes. Heat. And serve. Just like out of a jar.

Basil, parsley and oregano might as well have been the names of Italian cities she'd never been to.

So, that was our dinner. And yes, it was awful. Thank God we had rugelach. At least we didn't go hungry.

The next morning, we were still completely snowed in. Our street untouched by plows. But four houses away, 120th Ave. had been plowed. It was open to traffic. Though void of cars.

Everyone in our house grabbed shovels and started to dig the taxi out. Neighbors came out and joined in with their shovels. Together we dug a path to the plowed avenue. About 200 ft.

It took half the day. It was fun and hard work.

Richard's taxi started right up. He loaded his wife and child in and slowly backed down the street. Everyone out there grabbed onto the cab and pushed. Until he was on the avenue. And on his way home.

There is nothing like New Yorkers during a crisis. Everyone pulling and pushing together. But by spring, we would be back to ignoring each other once again.

Twelve years and twelve days later, I was living in my own little house. In Bloomfield. A working-class suburb of Hartford. With my wife and two baby boys both under two years of age.

These little guys were still in diapers. The cycle from full belly to full diaper repeated itself every few hours. They crapped like champs.

It was a typical winter day. We went about our business unaware of the impending catastrophe that would soon unfold.

I came home early that afternoon. Just as it started to snow. Within an hour the gentle flakes turned into an unrelenting storm. The snow kept coming.

It was then that my wife – her timing always exquisite – announced that we were out of diapers. My car was already piled with snow. And our streets were not yet plowed.

Connecticut Governor Ella Grasso had just declared a state of emergency. All roads were ordered closed. Except for emergencies.

That left me with a difficult choice. Obey the woman in the governor's mansion. Or the woman with whom I shared a bed. And who was melting down by the minute.

I thought about cutting my t-shirts into diapers. But we could be stuck for a couple of days. And I didn't own enough T-shirts.

Sorry governor, I'm going to listen to the wife.

In those days I drove a tank of a car. With enough miles on it to have circled the earth more than a couple of times. But it was high off the ground and could easily plow through a foot of snow.

I skidded out of the driveway and onto the unplowed streets.

There was a convenience store a mile away. I headed for it feeling a little like Dr. Zhivago fighting his way through a Siberian winter.

Thankfully no other cars were out. I skidded down the road like a Norwegian slalom skier.

As I pulled into the parking lot I was met with the blue lights of Bloomfield's finest. The officer stepped out of his car.

"What the hell are you doing out here, buddy? The governor closed the roads."

"Yeah, except for emergencies," I said. *"I've got two babies at home shitting their brains out. And I need more diapers."*

"Well, that's too bad. Pull out of here and get home," he commanded.

"Officer, you can arrest me, or you can shoot me, but please don't send me home without diapers. My wife does not handle disasters well. And when she goes nuts, she can be more than a little scary. And you don't want the paperwork from a domestic disturbance. Please. I'm begging you. I just need a quick minute or two."

He broke into a broad smile and waved me into the convenience store which was getting ready to close. I grabbed the remaining boxes of Pampers, and a gallon of milk, and was on my way in a minute flat.

It was a good call going out then to get diapers. The blizzard raged for three more days. Arctic winds created white-out conditions. Snow drifts reached as high as 15 feet. It took many days to clear all the streets.

The diapers I bought lasted until the roads were finally reopened.

My T-shirts were never put into service. And I never again complained about the heat of the summer.

12

CENTRAL PARK

Andrew Jackson High School operated largely in chaos. Some 4,000 noisy students had about five minutes at the end of each period to move through the school. And onto the next class of the day.

Teachers and administrators did their best to keep their eyes on the tidal wave of students flooding the hallways every hour.

All of this attention to safe passage meant that the front doors remained unsecured. When we wanted to, we simply walked out. Through the door. In full view. Like we had permission. No one ever stopped us.

Sometimes the plan of the day would be to simply cut out. Maybe spend the afternoon driving around. On a hot day maybe we'd head for the beach. Or to Shea Stadium if the Mets had an afternoon game.

But I think my favorite place to cut school was Central Park. A carload of us would scoot out after second period and meet at my car.

We'd pile in and drive 15 minutes to the subway stop in Jamaica on 169th St. It was easy to find parking on one of the side streets back then.

We would then grab the F train. Popping up from underground some 20 minutes later. A short walk and by about 10 am we'd be in the best urban park in the world.

Central Park.

843 acres of fun stuff to do in the middle of New York City. What better way to spend an otherwise boring day of high school.

How nice it was to have all the freedom in the world.

Our first stop would be at the lake. We would rent row boats just when they opened. Six guys. Three row boats.

We'd row into the middle of the lake. Then lay down in the boats to look at the puffy clouds. A few minutes later there would invariably be a water fight. No one was ever sure how it started. But we would drench each other splashing water with our oars.

And we'd laugh ourselves silly.

Eventually the boat guy, would blow a whistle and make us come in.

Next stop would be to stretch out on one of the large flat rocks lining the shore. This was good for getting us dry. The late morning sun warmed us up.

On one of our Central Park *cut days* we were laying out on the big rock. One of the guys said there was a cop walking down the patch.

"Don't worry. If he stops to ask us why we're here, tell him that we have the day off from parochial school. Tell him it's St. Eric's day. Catholics have saints days for just about everyone," I said.

"Eric. The cop is your dad."

Holy crap. It was my father. Not 20 feet from me. Walking by in uniform. There I was smoking a cigarette with my buddies in Central Park in the middle of the school day.

It is impossible to calculate the odds of my father walking past me at this very moment. In the middle of one of the largest cities in the world.

How do things like this even happen?

My father who never missed anything simply glanced over and walked right past us. Like he never even saw us.

I once read that when you see something so out of place it can somehow simply not register on a conscious level. This was the case for native Americans when they first saw boats come in from far off the coast.

I only hoped that this would be the case with my dad. Or. He just might kill me.

We scrambled away before he had a chance to turn around and double-check what he might have just seen.

For the record, my dad never said a word about seeing us in the park. We were, for all intents and purposes, invisible.

After a lunch of hot dogs and fries, we headed to our next stop. The Central Park Zoo. Where we roared with the lions and tigers trying to get them to roar back.

We mimicked the seals. And then scared ourselves silly in the Reptile House. Pretending a poisonous snake had escaped and slithered out.

But the most fun on this day was the Monkey House.

The zoo had a monkey that didn't like people very much. In fact, if you made too much noise, he would throw his feces at you.

A shit-throwing monkey to play with. Oh what fun!

The game was to enter the Monkey House and make some annoying monkey sounds. To in, you had to touch the far side of the building. And get back without getting monkey shit thrown at you.

We took turns. I recall I insisted on going first. Not because I am braver. Or faster. I simply figured that the monkey would be a little less irritated. And I was right.

The third one of us to run the gauntlet got the full ire of the shit-throwing monkey. I'll bet you didn't know that monkeys, at least this one anyway, are ambidextrous. He could throw shit both left and right-handed.

At the time, I thought the Mets could probably use a pitcher like this.

We laughed into giddy exhaustion. And headed back to the subway to take us home.

Remembering the fine words of Mark Twain.

"Don't let schooling get in the way of your education." We didn't.

13

SEALED WITH A KISS

To paraphrase Robert Duvall's line from the movie *Apocalypse Now* "I love the smell of driveway sealer in the morning."

How that scent brings me back to my carefree teenage years. And also to one of the worst days of my young life.

An enterprising high school buddy, Frank, and I would go door to door offering to squeegee down driveway sealer. It was a great job for kids not yet 18.

Each weekend morning, we'd put as many 5-gallon drums of the thick black goop that could fit in the trunk of my thirteen-year-old Plymouth.

The car squeaked and groaned complaining in the only way it knew at the added weight. With each bump the bottom of the vehicle scraped on the road.

But I knew that with each stop the weight would lighten. As we began to offload the buckets of black goop we used to spread on customers' driveways. We'd clear $40 for every job.

Off we went to the neighboring communities of Valley Stream, Lynbrook and the Five Towns, the nouveau riche Long Island towns closest to us. Homes in our neighborhood had cement driveways that last forever.

But in our target-rich environment of Long Island, most of the homes had asphalt driveways. Which deteriorate after some years.

Frank was chubby and had a baby face. He did the door knocking. He looked less intimidating than me. And his closure rate was pretty good.

As we were finishing one driveway, he'd scurry along down the block to scare up new business.

On a good Saturday, we could knock off as many as four or five driveways. Those were the days when the minimum wage was $1.30 an hour.

So we made good money that spring. And then opportunity struck. The distributor who sold us the driveway sealer had a job for us.

The Atlantic Beach and Tennis Club needed their six tennis courts sealed. He would deliver the product to the site and pay us $300 for the work. All we had to do was show up with our brooms, squeegees and strong backs.

How hard could that be for such a big payday?

Since neither of us had ever actually stepped onto a tennis court, we had no idea how large they were. Our distributor had delivered eight large barrel drums of the thick green goop and left a two-word note.

Good Luck!

Each barrel was 55 gallons. We could barely move them since they were more than ten times the size and weight of what we were used to.

We contemplated just getting in my car and leaving. But in 1969, $300 for a day's work was a small fortune.

To compound the complexities of the job, these barrels needed to be stirred. The thick, goopy product at the bottom had to be mixed with the runny green, liquid at the top.

I grabbed a couple of stickball bats from the trunk of my car while Frank figured out how to pry the top off the first barrel.

Frank swept the first of six courts while I began to stir the thick green goop.

Using a trial-and-error method (mostly error) we eventually figured out how to pour small amounts of liquid onto the court. And began to spread it.

By the time we finished the first court, we were covered in the green goop. Only five more courts to go.

Did I mention that this was my birthday? June 21st. The longest day of the year. The day I turned 18.

It was also very hot. So I took off my shirt. I'd like to say I looked like the Incredible Hulk since I was all covered in green. But to be honest, I looked more like a skinny Martian who crash-landed at a Long Island beach club.

Under the cloudless sky, the sun beat down relentlessly. Now you might ask if I had sunscreen lotion. Of course not. I was 18 and was going to live forever. I was as strong as an ox. And, on this day, about as stupid.

We finished the job late that afternoon. Dehydrated, sunburned with aching muscles. I had no idea how I was going to remove the green thick slime covering every bit of my exposed body.

My sunburn was epic. I looked like a large spinach pizza fresh from the oven.... hot, red, and green.

It was a terribly painful ride home. I thought about the $150 I just made for a long day of labor. But it just made me feel worse. It just wasn't enough money to be in this much pain.

I arrived home to a Carvel Ice Cream birthday cake. Lit with candles left over from Chanukah. (My family never could count very well.) At least they remembered that Carvel was my favorite cake.

I just wanted to rub the ice cream cake all over me and sleep for a week. My family sang an out-of-tune "Happy Birthday" as my grandmother applied butter to my sunburn. Right then and there I felt like I was going to die.

To cheer me up my mother handed me a few birthday cards that came in the mail.

Mixed in with the cards was a letter that immediately caught my attention. It was from the US Selective Service Agency – my fucking Draft Board! – reminding me it is a Federal violation not to register with the agency upon turning 18.

I burned my draft card my first semester in college. But to be honest, it was less of a political statement than it seems. I was just trying to impress a girl who was burning her bra.

Gotta love the 1960's.

Horrifyingly, that was the year 16,899 Americans returned from Vietnam in body bags. The most of any year of the war.

I suppose I should be thankful that all I got hit with was a particularly nasty sunburn.

14

MY LITTLE SISTER

I was five years old and had hoped for a little brother. A little guy I could teach stuff to.

What I got was Amy. What the hell was I going to do with her? She's a girl.

She looked like the kid on the Campbell's soup can. Adorable. With big blue eyes and dirty blonde hair. But for the first couple of years of her life, she didn't do anything interesting. But cry and fill up her diaper.

Everyone made a big fuss over her. She was the first girl in the family. My father called her his *little flower* as he danced across the room with her in his arms singing "Once in Love with Amy, " a popular song of his day.

Andy and I rolled our eyes. Now when I hear that song my eyes get a little misty.

Dolls, frilly clothes, and pink stuff came into our house.

About the time she turned five, I began to see her as a little person. With her own identity and personality.

To me she was pretty cool but lacked my worldly experience. Let's face it, I was all grown up by then – at least in my mind.

I was ten and in the fourth grade.

I told her then that I'd take care of her. And that no one would ever mess with my little sister.

One night she and I teamed up to babysit for our brand-new baby brother, Tom. He was three weeks old. My parents had taken Andy out to dinner for his 12th birthday leaving me in charge.

Yes, had that been today Social Services would have taken us away from my parents. And found us a safer home. But this was the 1960s when kids played in the streets. There were no seat belts. And everyone, including doctors, smoked.

So there we were, Amy and me. Tom was asleep in his crib right up until the moment my parents pulled the old station wagon out of the driveway.

He woke up screaming. So I picked him up and walked him around singing the only song I knew, "Take Me Out to the Ballgame."

I guess he didn't like baseball very much because that only seemed to piss him off even more. His cries grew louder. Amy and I determined that he must be hungry. So we lit the old gas stove. And heated up a bottle of milk. Just like we'd seen my mother do.

After about ten minutes of his screaming, we got the temperature just right. And I shoved the bottle into my howling brother's mouth.

We guessed right as Tom gulped down the bottle of warm milk like a fraternity brother gulps down cold beer.

"Now you have to burp him," Amy said, as she directed me how to do that.

We walked him around some more until he started to sleep.

And then I smelled it. His diaper was full. Amy insisted that I change him. Which I refused to do.

I returned my smelly brother to his crib. And swore Amy to a secret we have kept to this day.

When my parents came home, I said, *"He smelled fine when I put him down, Mom."*

Years later I was wearing my grandmother's flapper dress. No, stop thinking that. I was going to a high school Halloween party. In drag.

My mother had a couple of wigs which a lot of moms had back then. I grabbed one from her closet – without permission, of course.

Honestly, I was kind of cute. That was many years before I grew a mustache.

"Now you need makeup," my ten-year-old sister said. Not the first or the last time Amy would roll her eyes at me. Or boss me around.

She grabbed a bunch of makeup from my mother's dresser and applied it on me.

Now I looked like a cross between a down-on-her-luck streetwalker and a circus clown. I was also wearing sneakers. I surely would have broken an ankle attempting to walk in heels.

Later that night as I was walking home a couple of neighborhood boys shouted insulting comments to me from their front porch. I took offense at their misogynist comments. Even though I didn't know at the time what a misogynist was.

In a very unladylike gesture, I pulled off my wig and said something like *"You want a piece of me. Come on down here and I'll knock your heads together you little bastards."*

I suppose it was then that I became a feminist. After all, I had a little sister to look out for.

A few years later I taught Amy and her 15-year-old friends how to drink tequila. Salt. A shot of tequila. And then suck on a slice of lime. My parents were not at all happy.

I spent the summer of my sophomore year of college in Hartford. Amy was 16, working as a camp counselor in the Berkshires. An hour and a half away. On her day off she and a friend, in halter top blouses and hotpants, hitchhiked down to visit me.

I did not live in a particularly nice or safe neighborhood. When she and her friend showed up unannounced, I hit the roof.

"Are you out of your frigging mind? What the hell were you thinking?" I shouted as the vein in my forehead bulged.

This was the same line my father used on me whenever I did something stupid.

After a quick lunch, my roommate and I squished them both into the rear seat of his tiny car. And returned them back to summer camp. We kept that incident from our parents. Or surely, they would have dragged her home.

Amy had a part-time job in high school as a cashier at the local supermarket. My first wife and I lived nearby on Long Island at the time. So we shopped a few times at her supermarket.

Amy knew we were close to broke. When we brought our groceries to her register, she rang up dramatically lower prices. This was before bar codes and scanners.

I felt guilty about enjoying a $12 roast we paid $1.20 for. So we started to shop elsewhere. Somehow my dad found out and as you can imagine he predictably shouted, *"Are you out of your frigging mind? What the hell were you thinking?"*

The vein on his forehead bulged too.

Some years later she and her fiancé, Alan, visited me in Connecticut. It was winter and we decided to go skiing. Alan was a good skier. Neither Amy nor I knew how to ski. But that didn't stop us.

Off to the ski slope we went. We rented the equipment. And signed up for beginner lessons. While my future brother-in-law enjoyed racing down the black diamond trail.

For an hour, our instructor Klaus directed us. Once he thought we were ready, he took us to the chairlift. He said in his thick German accent – almost bragging, *"All you must do is stand up when the lift gets to the top. Nobody falls down with Klaus."*

The three of us got on the chairlift together. When we hit the top, Amy and I stood up and immediately fell on poor Klaus. Stabbing him multiple times with our ski poles. The lesson was over.

He took our ski poles away. We somehow made it down to the bottom of the hill without them. Mostly on our asses.

From the parking lot we looked back to see the bunny hill we conquered that day. The mountain behind it – which we never attempted – was huge by comparison. But tiny if put next to the more seriously sized ski resorts of Vermont or Colorado.

Neither of us ever skied again. But we often laugh at the time we nearly turned poor Klaus into a shish kabob.

Amy and Alan were married the following year. Just prior to their ceremony I celebrated their nuptials with a cocktail on an empty stomach.

I had also taken an allergy pill as my hay fever was acting up. To make this a perfect storm my rented tuxedo shirt was too tight around my neck. And, of course, it was an unusually warm September afternoon.

I held a corner of the chuppah under which the bride and groom shared their vows. And became woozy.

Before Amy could say *"I do"* down I went. I was OK after a couple of minutes. Forced to watch the remainder of the wedding ceremony from a front-row seat.

I felt two powerful emotions. First, I was so very proud of my little sister. She had grown into a wonderful woman, loving and caring. And she chose a man who I was and still am honored to call my brother.

Second, I felt horrible, having ruined the most important day thus far of my sister's life.

From a very young age, every little girl dreams about her wedding day. When all eyes are on her. It is *her* special day. And I felt I wrecked it.

At the conclusion of the ceremony, I gave Amy a hug and told her how sorry I was.

True to her essence, she said something like *"So long as you are OK my day is perfect. Now let's party, brother."*

It was at that moment when I realized that we take care of each other. That was 40 years ago. Amy and I remain very close. We speak at least once a week. And when we are together – which is never often enough – there is laughter and joy.

Honestly, there is much to criticize about our parents and their child-rearing skills. But somehow, Andy, Amy, Tom and I survived and thrived. They must have done something right.

15

— • —

SID

He stood about six feet two inches tall and weighed in at well over 200 lbs. of solid muscle. He looked a bit like a slab of granite. With a square face and a marine flat top haircut.

His name was Sid. I would say that he was my dad's best friend. More accurately he was my dad's only friend.

My dad had a lot of family he enjoyed. But few, if any, friends. My mother was typically in charge of their modest social calendar. But Sid was all his.

Sid and Zelda lived a few blocks away. Their kids were roughly the same age as the four of us. So we hung out a lot. They were a lot like cousins.

Sid was a former high school football star. Well into his middle years, he looked like he could still play.

He was also a cop. And he took crap from no one.

Their house was on the corner of 121st Ave. An extra wide avenue divided by a raised median strip. Standing on the avenue facing Manhattan, just 6 miles away, one could clearly see the Empire State Building – then, the tallest building in the world.

This was an ideal place to drag race. As there were two wide lanes on each side of the median strip.

As the story goes, the drag races commenced one night. This time Sid was at home. Cursing a bit under his breath he went to the garage and brought a 2x4 out to the corner.

The cars revved their engines. A pretty girl – always a pretty girl – waved the start flag. And the cars took off at a high rate of speed toward where he was standing.

Sid threw the 2x4 in the middle of the road. And stood there on the corner with his hands on his hips. Daring the dragsters to get out of their cars.

The drivers braked their cars to a quick stop. Took one look at this monster on the corner. And threw their cars into reverse. That was the end of drag racing on 121st Ave.

But when I think of Sid, the story that comes to mind the clearest is his son Barry's Bar Mitzvah. Not the service. But the party afterward.

Barry was the same age as my sister Amy. They were inseparable elementary school friends.

I was 18, five years older. And a college man. I think many of my parents' friends were surprised that I actually found a school to accept me. But that's a story for another day.

It was a hot, humid July afternoon. I was sweating on the car ride over to the banquet hall. The parking lot was pretty full. Both of the facility's two banquet halls were booked with parties. They shared a common entrance.

I had just completed my freshman year. So I strolled into the party with the stride of an invincible young man. I was hoping to take a shot at a family friend whom I hadn't seen since high school.

She graduated a year ahead of me. And hadn't lost anything in the looks department.

The entire facility was filled with lit candles. At first, I thought, "How romantic!" My second thought was that this massive display of candles sure heated up the space. Which was already uncomfortably warm.

Who decorates a banquet facility like this in early July? A dumb move, I thought.

In those days power would go out regularly. Blackouts. Brownouts. And sometimes an unexplained outage.

It took a while for me to realize that the power was indeed out. No one looked like they were in a Bar Mitzvah dancing mood.

Thankfully, I was seated at a table with the object of my desire and Barry's older sisters. It would have been truly awful to sit with my parents.

But the young woman I had hoped to make an impression on never gave me a second look. Not a first one either. She was still out of my league. College man or not, it felt just like high school.

An hour into the party I got up to stretch my legs. And try to air out my armpits which at this point were feeling a tad swampy.

I noticed Sid standing at the door. Seething. This was not the look of a happy man.

I saw three couples from the other party in the building trying to sneak into our party for free drinks. The guys looked to be in their mid-thirties. They too were uncomfortably warm and bored.

Sid stepped in front of them. And asked where they thought they were going. The smallest of the three – it is always the smallest – put his finger in his glass. And flicked some liquid in Sid's face.

This did not cool Sid off.

Like the star lineman he was in high school, Sid pushed the three guys through the front door in one swift motion. I quickly followed behind him like a tailback.

A few more of their friends joined in, along with a very loud-mouthed woman. A drunk woman with a big mouth rarely calms things down.

Words were exchanged. And Sid exploded, flooring one of the guys with a roundhouse blow. I did my best to have Sid's back. But I don't think he needed much help.

One of the guys cold-cocked me with a shot to my face. A glancing blow. Which did more to piss me off than hurt me.

I hit him with two quick left jabs. And a pretty strong right cross to his face.

I only hoped his face hurt more than my fist. Because my hand hurt like hell.

That's the thing about street fights. The hands hurt first. Somehow getting punched in the face doesn't hurt until much later. I like to think of it as adrenaline-rewarding stupidity.

With a few punches thrown and a lot of angry words spoken, my dad and some other men separated everyone. Cooler heads prevailed.

My dad flipped open his wallet and showed his badge. This calmed everyone down.

Someone said the cops were called. My father took Sid for a ride away from the scene so he wouldn't get arrested. When punches get thrown you never can tell who ends up in the pokey.

It would have been bad form for the Bar Mitzvah boy's father to be hauled off in cuffs. Even though it was the little putz from the party next door who had started the fracas.

After dropping Sid off somewhere a few minutes away my dad came back to speak with the local cops. He let them know that he too was *on the job* – cop talk for we're on the same team. And everything settled down.

No one pressed charges. Or needed medical attention. Sid returned to the party. And things got back to normal.

I could feel a bruise on my cheek forming as I reentered the party. I thought this might impress the young lady. It did not.

So I joined in on the second fracas of the day. Fighting to get through the crowd to the enormous dessert buffet. Overflowing with an astonishing array of sweet treats.

Don't ever get caught between a mob of elderly Jews and the Viennese table at a Bar Mitzvah. It is safer to be in a parking lot brawl with angry drunks.

A bit later in the afternoon Sid and I made eye contact. From across the room, he smiled at me and gave me a nod. I smiled back and gave him a shrug.

I always liked that guy.

16

TILL THE FAT LADY SINGS

I was in the middle of a dating dry spell. So I decided to take myself to the opera. Just me. And *Carmen*. On a Saturday night in Hartford.

There is usually a single ticket available. And sure enough, they had one for me in the upper deck. In opera parlance – the rear balcony.

I was seated two rows from the back at Bushnell Auditorium. A 90-year-old, four-thousand-seat performance center. Modeled after Radio City Music Hall.

Its Art Deco ceiling is a thing of beauty. And I ought to know as I was pretty close to it.

A middle-aged guy sat down next to me. He wore a Detroit Tigers baseball cap on his balding head. A gigantic pair of binoculars hung from his neck. He looked like he was going to the racetrack rather than the opera. He was there alone too.

"My wife hates this shit," he said. *"I love it. So I'm fine coming here by myself. Carmen is my favorite."*

I suddenly felt more at ease being there solo. We chatted a bit until the lights dimmed. I borrowed his binoculars a few times to get a close-up view of some of the action.

Carmen was a delight. It was easy to follow. I even recognized a few of the arias.

I've always liked live theater. And have been a lifelong fan of classical music. Opera combined the two into one magical experience.

Norma, whom I would meet a few years later and eventually marry, was seated in the orchestra that night. It was her teenage daughter Alex's first opera, too.

Years later, Norma and I subscribed to the Connecticut Opera. Four times a year we'd look forward to attending. We had great seats so we could easily read the supertitles. Without which we'd have no clue what was going on.

We enjoyed the experience so much, that I put my name on the list to be a supernumerary. That's a guy who fills in empty spaces on the stage.

He might walk on stage carrying a spear. Or help carry off the fallen after a battle scene. He neither sings nor gets paid. I always thought that would be a lot of fun. But they never called.

Which reminds me of the story:

There was a dentist who was given one line in an amateur opera production. On cue, he is to walk on stage and deliver the line *"Hark, I hear the cannons roar."* For the weeks leading up to the production he practices and practices the delivery of his one line. With each delivery, he accents different syllables. *"Hark I hear the cannons roar – Hark I hear the cannons roar."* You get the picture. The night of the performance he is dressed in the full military regalia of the times. He is quite nervous. On cue, he steps on stage to the deafening sound of a cannon blast.

And he shouts, *"What the fuck was that?"*

Though we enjoyed most of the operas we saw, to be honest, a few did suck a little.

The soprano in the fourth act of La Traviata kept getting up off the floor to sing again and again before finally dying. Like the corner man at a boxing match. I wanted to throw a towel and shout for her to *stay down*. It was late. Three hours deep into the opera and I was ready to go home.

And then there was the opera Hansel and Gretel. It was not sung in beautiful French or Italian. They sang it in English which offended my eardrums. Also, Hansel had boobs. Really. All too much for me. We left at half-time. In opera parlance, intermission.

Interestingly, Norma was named after the lead character in the opera *Norma*. Her oldest brother Pepe – her godfather – was an opera singer in Mexico City.

As with so many regional arts organizations, the Connecticut Opera went broke. It is incredibly expensive to stage live operas.

Years went by without our giving opera another thought. And then through the miracle of high definition via satellite simulcast, The Metropolitan Opera began transmitting live performances at digital movie theaters worldwide.

It is incredible to experience world-class operas at our local movie theater. At an affordable price. All that plus very cushy seating, popcorn, and, of course, Raisinets.

Admittedly, I've been known to take a brief opera nap from time to time. But I do that in most movie theaters, anyway. And it takes nothing away from really enjoying this experience.

As the man once said, *"The opera ain't over till the fat lady sings."*

17

THE DATING LIFE

I don't like autumn very much. It's the season when everything starts to die. Soon to be buried in a deep frost. Forgotten until the robin sings.

It was autumn when my fifteen-year marriage finally ran out of steam. Leaving me with a heavily mortgaged house and two rambunctious pre-teen boys.

We agreed for her to take pretty much whatever modest assets we had.

All I really wanted was custody of the boys and the deed to the only home they knew.

And, of course, my freedom from an unhappy marriage.

The Janis Joplin lyric, "*Freedom's just another word for nothing left to lose,*" often rolled around in my head in those days.

With nothing left to lose, I was ready to embark on a new life.

The thought of dating was a bit terrifying. I hadn't had a date in four presidents. And I didn't know where to begin.

I'd never been a pick 'em up easy guy. I wasn't very smooth. I had no game with the ladies. I am also a bit shy.

So, there I was a middle-aged divorcee with two kids at home. I had a wardrobe full of *dad* clothes. A bad haircut. And six-pack abs that had matured into a quarter keg.

Admittedly, not a great catch. I wondered if I was destined to spend the rest of my years in solitude.

The last time I felt this alone was when I spent an afternoon lost in Manhattan. I was four. I survived that. So I suppose I'd survive this.

Time to put on my big boy pants. And start a new adventure.

I was as uncomfortable as you can be walking into a singles bar on a Thursday night in West Hartford. The chatter was palpable. Increasing in volume as I stepped in.

I immediately felt I was being sized up. Like a prisoner entering the exercise yard for the first time. *Fresh meat.* The white band on my ring finger gave away most of my secrets.

Over the next hour, I sipped a pinot grigio or two. I spoke with no one. And finally went home. Lonely and dejected.

I asked the women in my office for some advice. Not surprisingly, they had a lot to offer. The consensus was that most men in their 30s are immature, assholes, or both. *Just be honest about who you are and what you want in life. And you'll do fine.*

For the next dozen years, I was successfully single. I met incredible women having interesting lives. In learning about them, I discovered a great deal about myself.

Of course, there were more than a few whack jobs along the way.

One loved to watch and talk about professional wrestling.

Another was *born again* with a personal mission to convert Jewish men to her brand of Christianity. Still another tried to get me into a bar fight. She said bloody men turned her on.

Then there was the one who boasted about being a descendant of the Pilgrims on the Mayflower. Which she mentioned as often as possible. She was not impressed at all that my family also came by boat from Europe. Steerage class through Ellis Island.

I dated several different women who were clearly raised by wolves. I've never been a stickler on manners. But for heaven's sake, don't talk with your mouth full of food. And close the bathroom door when you pee.

And who could ever forget the psycho therapist? Yes, that would be *two* words. She was quite nuts.

Another was on a serious husband hunt. She was from somewhere in Eastern Europe. And overstayed her visa. When I think about her pouty face and injected lips the name *Resting Bitchface* comes to mind.

I also dated a lovely woman who used the expression *not for nothing* in almost every sentence she uttered. Forcing me to the exit door. Admittedly, this does make me sound shallow enough to be in a Seinfeld episode, don't you think?

I was told by friends that I had become a serial dater. Naturally, I thought it meant sleeping over. And having Frosted Flakes for breakfast.

My goal in dating was simply to share time with interesting people. At that time in my life, I had no interest in getting married or having more children.

Over these years I came to accept that I was fine on my own. With many wonderful platonic women friends.

I found that my women friends offered insights and perspectives that differ from those of my male friends. My female friends provided me with more honest feedback. And constructive criticism from a different point of view.

Having women as platonic friends also helped me improve my communication skills. Learning how to better express myself effectively and respectfully, has proven to be valuable in both personal and professional relationships.

I frankly wasn't looking and didn't expect to get serious with anyone.

And then Norma showed up in my life. At this writing, we've been together for over 20 years. Each year continues to be better than the last.

She has also become friends with my women friends.

My 12 years of single life taught me a great deal about myself. As I continue on my path to becoming a better man.

But I still don't like autumn very much.

18

— • —

TODAY I AM A MAN

Put a few dozen pubescent young men in their only sport coats on a Saturday morning and what do you have?

Another Bar Mitzvah.

Since ancient times when a Jewish boy reaches the age of 13 – middle-aged in those days – he is called to the bema (the podium up front) and is asked to read a small passage from the Torah. Along with some other prayers. And he then delivers a speech letting everyone in his life know that he is now a man.

It often surprises me how many people don't know that The Torah is simply the first five books in the Old Testament. Just written on a scroll. In Hebrew. Made even more difficult as it is written without any vowels.

Imagine reading this sentence without any vowels.

Imgne rdng ths sntnc wtht ny vwls. There would be a lot of guesswork.

To make matters worse, there are little squiggly notations around the Hebrew letters guiding the reader on how to chant it. Perhaps the earliest form of written music.

Yes, the Bar Mitzvah boy chants his section – 10 of the longest minutes of a boy's short life – to a large room full of family and friends. It can be a horror show for the boy. Bad for everyone's ears. But quite often funny as hell.

The nervousness and vocal changes – sometimes mid-note – from a pubescent young man often results in a room full of smiles. And an occasional guffaw.

At some point during elementary school Jewish boys – since the 1950s girls too – attend Hebrew school. Usually, one afternoon a week as well as on Saturday morning. There he or she learns how to read Hebrew and prepare for his Bar or her Bat Mitzvah.

I wrote about my own Bar Mitzvah experience in my first book, **Harry Would Be So Proud**. Plenty to laugh about there.

But this story is about being the father of my two boys and their unusual Bar Mitzvahs.

Their mother and I had recently divorced. We were able to call a cease-fire. And not make our oldest son Jason's Bar Mitzvah the battlefield for our unresolved marital issues.

I rented the ballroom at the Avon Old Farms Hotel. A bit fancy for my meager budget. But I have a large family. Perhaps out of the guilt of not having an intact primary family unit, I told Jason to invite whatever friends he would like. He did. He invited everyone he knew.

Popular kid. He nearly broke me.

The service went off without a hitch. I asked a grumpy old member of the congregation to serve as the *Heysedonda*. His job was to patrol the back of the sanctuary where dozens of Jason's friends sat. When required he sternly shouted, *"Hey! Sit down there,"* in his Brooklyn-Yiddish accent.

Toward the end of the service the father – that would be me – and the son – that would be Jason – marched around the synagogue carrying the Torah. It is the tradition among Eastern European Jews to gently toss candy in celebration of this sweet time as a boy becomes a man.

Many of Jason's friends were from his baseball team. More than happy to show off their strong arms. Pelting us with hard candies. I'm not sure which covenant of Judaism I broke by blocking the hard candies with the Torah I was carrying. But I didn't want to lose an eye.

The synagogue is a couple of miles from the hotel where the celebratory lunch was to be held. I needed to transport something like 30 kids. Luckily, I knew a guy who owned a limo company. And I called in a favor.

For the cost of renting a completely forgettable school bus, I rented a couple of stretch limos to transport the children to the party. This was their first ride in a limo. I rationalized the one-way trip was in lieu of a party favor. Which no one ever cares about anyway. This was a memorable experience.

As soon as the limos left the synagogue's driveway, the moon roof opened. Heads popped up. And napkins from the bar flew out trailing behind in the wind.

I was glad I had ample cash on me to over-tip the drivers. These kids were animals.

Finally, we all settled in for a nice party. And then general mayhem ensued. Once the dinner and dessert were served the kids snuck out of the ballroom. And ran through the corridors of the hotel.

They held bellhop cart races through the hallways. And turned over each *Do Not Disturb* sign to read *Please Make Up Room*.

When the party was over, I sat with the manager to settle the bill. Although there was no real damage done, he made it clear that we were not welcome back. Ever.

Whatever happened to the customer always being right?

A year later it was Jon's turn. As he approached his 13th birthday, he was very clear. *"I ain't doing this shit,"* he said.

I had been under tremendous stress. Managing the lives of a couple of teenagers as a single parent, along with my own health crisis. I also knew that I would soon be out of work.

I did not have it in me to force the issue as I was just barely hanging on myself. I told Jon that someday if he wanted a Bar Mitzvah, I would be happy to pay for a luncheon. For him and his friends to celebrate the occasion.

And that was the end of that. For seventeen years.

Jon began studying for his Bar Mitzvah as he neared his 30th birthday. Better late than never, I suppose.

And so, in his 30th year, he was called up to the bema to read his Torah portion. And officially become a man in our tradition.

He made it through the Hebrew chanting. And did it surprisingly well. I was so proud of him. But that is not what was memorable.

As I mentioned earlier, Bar Mitzvah boys give a speech to describe how they feel about entering adulthood. And to thank all those who helped prepare him for this special moment.

To be clear, Jon is the funniest person I know. At the time he was working toward becoming a stand-up comic. He now had a mike in his hand. And a captive audience.

What could possibly go wrong?

I would not do justice trying to recall all that he had to say that day. He walked the fine line of inappropriateness. And he was flat-out funny. Leaving his family and friends doubled over with laughter.

The rest of the congregation was horrified. Mouths agape, heads shaking, left to wonder who these Litsky people were.

That's my family.

His speech concluded with, *"Finally, I'd like to thank the Rabbi for his time and patience preparing me for this special day. I'd like you to know that I won't be here for the next Friday night service. I have a date. And if it goes well, I won't be here Saturday morning either."*

Don't get me wrong. Though we are not a particularly religious family, we are proud to be Jewish. We just often have a funny way of showing it.

19

PHYSICAL THERAPY

The calf on my leg hurt for several weeks. I thought it might have been Karma. As my favorite meal is veal parmesan.

Wrong calf.

My doctor ordered a scan to make sure that it was not DVT – deep vein thrombosis – which could severely mess you up. Particularly if you fly a lot. And we like to travel.

The scan was done. I was in the clear. But my leg still hurt. So off to physical therapy I went.

No one in physical therapy is happy to be there. Except, that is, for the overly healthy physical therapists in yoga pants with matching logoed t-shirts.

If you are new to physical therapy, it is a large room filled with all sorts of devices designed to torture you. An earlier version of the apparatus I was put on may have originated during the Spanish Inquisition.

My therapist was Joan. She was a recent graduate full of new knowledge, energy, and a desire to heal. She spoke quickly. In upspeak. After a little warm-up she had me stretch using different color bands. *"Now give me 3 sets of 10 with the blue ones. Then four sets with the green ones holding each for 20 seconds. And then finish up with 3 sets of 5 holding for 10 seconds,"* she said more quickly than I could grasp.

In all fairness, she also didn't know that I am challenged with some form of color blindness. I asked her to repeat her instructions a couple of times. Then I shrugged my shoulders. And I did what I wanted. When it hurt, I went on just a tad bit longer. Afterward, she stretched me out. Which is a good thing to do. That is unless you had eaten chili the night before. I do love my chili. Of course, when she pulled on my leg. I farted. It was audible. But thankfully not stinky. *"I guess that my calf muscle was not the only thing tight this morning,"* I said.

I often joke to hide my awkwardness. Those within an earshot heard both my fart as well as my comment. The place broke out in a few smiles. Everyone in physical therapy is so appropriate and polite. A few weeks of $40 copays later there was not much measurable progress. They suggested something called a dry needle. Placing a needle into the muscle to get it to relax. To me that was counterintuitive. It made no sense.

In my head, I heard, *"Let's shove a big old needle into that charley horse of yours."* Not mine! I answered with a polite but firm, *"No thank you."*

I also discovered that my leg has excellent hearing. At the mere suggestion of a needle, the pain in my calf quickly disappeared. I think she simply scared the pain away. I wish she had mentioned that during the first session.

I need to get myself back to the gym. My insurance company pays for a membership. It's about a mile from my house. One of those 24-hour franchises I can access any time with the fob I have on my keyring. There is no excuse for not going.

It is open every day except Christmas. Jews don't go to the gym on Christmas anyway. We eat Chinese food.

So, I will go back to the gym. And lift stuff up. And put stuff down. And ride a stationary bike to nowhere. And walk up and down hills for miles on a treadmill. Breathing recirculated gym air.

I've never found going to the gym to be much fun. But it certainly has to be better than the embarrassment of farting in physical therapy.

20

FOR THE BIRDS

There I was hanging out of a second-story window in my underwear. Trying to shoot a bird with my kid's super soaker water gun.

My neighbor gave me an uncomfortable wave of his hand. He got into his car and headed off to work. I don't think he really wanted to know what I was doing.

While dragging my garbage can to the end of the driveway, I looked up to discover what was the clanking I heard each daybreak. It was a bird pecking on the metal cap of my chimney. Its echo vibrated as the noise pulsated through my house. Morning after morning it woke me up.

Initially, I thought my heating system needed to be serviced. Or that someone was trying to break in.

Time to take action. The next morning I was awakened once again to clanking. I quickly pumped up my water weapon, hung out of the window, and took aim. I was then rudely reacquainted with the concept of gravity.

Whatever water I shot up. Came straight back down. Right in my face. I don't know if a woodpecker is capable of laughter like Woody Woodpecker. But I'm pretty sure this one was smirking with delight.

I think I got him a little wet. Because that was the last time I saw him.

Some years later, Norma moved in. I had all but forgotten about the woodpecker caper. I like nature. Seeing critters of all kinds around my house makes me happy.

That is until the next spring. We were under attack. From *Kamikaze Bird*. That's what we named him. Each quiet afternoon he would dive bomb the living room bay window.

At first, I thought it was an errant throw from kids playing ball outside. But then I realized that kids don't play outside anymore. They have become indoor plants. Attached to their electronic devices of choice.

And then we saw it. A bird came straight for our bay window. Just like a WWII Kamikaze pilot.

He hit it hard. He bounced off. Shrugged his feathers. And flew off.

Thinking the bird saw his reflection in the window, Norma and I hung some netting I used in my garden. That made sense. But it didn't work. *Kamikaze Bird* dove again.

I then hung a large balloon with a huge owl's eye on it. The package said it was guaranteed to scare birds away. *Kamikaze Bird* laughed at it and dove once more. And again he bounced off the glass. And then flew off.

We kept adding things we thought would scare the bird away. Colorful streamers for the trees. Wind chimes. Stuffed animals. None of that worked.

Finally, we added several of our granddaughters' dolls onto the ledge of the bay window. But these little plastic people didn't work either.

A friend of ours stopped by. She did a double take when she saw all that we put in the window, and she said, *"Are you guys practicing voodoo?"*

With that, we surrendered. *Kamikaze Bird* had won. He was smarter than us. We removed everything we put up to scare him away. And just let nature do what nature does.

A few days later the attacks stopped. And we didn't hear from *Kamikaze Bird* again.

That is until the following spring. And each spring since.

We've gotten used to the occasional bang on our window from this crazy bird and his progeny. And we just smile.

I've become more mindful of birds lately. My father's favorite bird was the cardinal. My dad has been gone for almost a decade. But each time I see a red cardinal I think of him.

In addition to wild turkeys gobbling away in our yard each fall there is a wide assortment of birds loudly chirping each morning at daybreak. On occasion, a houseguest will ask if there is any way to turn down the birds.

"They don't come with remotes," is my only response.

One morning an emu strolled through my yard. Yes, an emu which is typically found in Australia. Not in Simsbury, CT. It is the second largest bird in the world. The ostrich is the largest.

I had heard that an emu escaped from a local petting zoo. And had been roaming around our suburban town for the last few months.

Eventually, this six foot 130 lbs. flightless bird found its way to my backyard. But of course, it did.

While watching it from our deck we quickly Googled some basic information as this odd bird made itself at home.

With its powerful legs, it can jump 7 feet off the ground. Sprint up to 30 mph. And kick the crap out of almost anything that poses a threat. Admiring it from a distance seemed like the best plan.

He also looked like Mr. Weiner. My 9th grade math teacher. Who happened not to like me very much. We sat quietly until it ambled off.

From my deck, I have a wonderful sky to look at as my house backs up to a game refuge. Most days there are hawks circling above. Occasionally one will land on a nearby tree. They are majestic creatures.

But my personal favorite is the tiniest of birds. The hummingbird. Through the summer months, they stop by to take nectar from our flowers.

In many indigenous cultures of the Americas, hummingbirds bring good intentions. If one flutters near you, it is believed that the bird carries positive messages to you from someone else in this world. Or in the afterworld.

When a hummingbird flutters by, I simply smile. And say thank you.

That is good enough for me.

21

THE PUTZ ON THE GREEN

It would not have been a good bet that either one of us would have survived his teenage years. But there we were. We did it. My youngest son, Jon, was finally turning 20.

What a ride it had been. I was a divorced dad trying to raise him and his older brother, Jason. Other than the usual teenage drama, Jason was launched in life. Attending a college out of state.

And then there was Jon. He pushed all of my buttons. He was a sweet kid with a great sense of humor. But in no hurry to grow up. Every day was a battle.

So, when the calendar page turned, I thought we both needed to celebrate. We made it. We both survived his teenage years.

He had recently taken up golf, a sport about which I knew very little. And never really cared for.

Chasing around a little white ball all day seemed to me like a dreadful waste of my time. But I loved my son. And I was proud he was finally growing up.

I offered to take him on a business trip with me to San Francisco. And buy him a round of golf at Pebble Beach. Yeah, that one. The one overlooking the Pacific Ocean. Where all the pro golfers you can name come to play.

It is one of the most famous and scenic golf courses in the world. Well known for its challenging layout. And spectacular views.

It is also crazy expensive. Something I should have researched before offering. But that is why you have credit cards. Jon was so excited.

Pebble Beach is a very big deal. Over the years it has hosted a half dozen U.S. Open Championships. It is rated the greatest public golf course in America by Golf Digest. Its 18 holes is what golfers dream about.

I'm more of a windmill and clown's mouth kind of golfer. You know – mini golf. But I respect the awe this place holds for millions of golfers worldwide.

As a gift, however, I was pretty certain I'd overshot.

We drove south from San Francisco arriving an hour early for our tee time. They paired us up with a couple of older guys.

Since Jon had no partner, I asked the golf pro if I could caddie for my son. More like chauffeur him around in a cool golf cart. He agreed and our foursome headed out for the first tee.

While the three guys took turns hitting the ball. I fantasized about what life must be like living in one of the gigantic homes, adjacent to the most spectacular golf course in the world. With ocean views to die for.

If you have to ask the price. You can't afford it.

But driving the cart was fun. I even handed Jon a club a few times. Although he had to tell me which club he wanted. Real caddies know which ones to pick. Based on the distance to the green and weather conditions. I had absolutely no feel for this game at all.

Our lovely day was nearing its close as I pulled up to the tee box for the famous 17th hole. A par 3 facing directly into the windy Pacific Ocean.

It is 177 yards from the tee to the hole. Not a very long shot. But quite challenging. There are sand traps on each side of the green. And if you hit the ball too hard it will end up in the ocean.

Jon had taken me to a driving range a few times. While he drove the golf ball around 300 yards, I could hit it regularly in the low 200s. But driving it into the unpredictable Pacific winds seemed to require much more luck than skill.

I've always been a lucky guy. And since we were never coming back, I figured I'd take my shot. Who knows? It could drop in. Now *that* would be a story I'd tell for the rest of my life. How jealous my golfer friends would be.

Visualizing a *hole in one* I grabbed one of Jon's clubs and quickly placed a ball on the tee.

A strong wind blew in, so I figured I'd have to hit it extra hard.

I swung. And I missed. The ball trickled off the tee. I grabbed it and sheepishly returned to our cart.

One of the old guys in the other cart shook his head from side to side.

"What a putz," was all I heard.

The Yiddish translation of *putz* is penis. But it is commonly used to describe a jerk, a fool, or an idiot.

So, I guess you could say that for a brief moment in time, I was the *putz* on the 17th green at Pebble Beach.

For the record, Jon went on to become a PGA teaching pro. And, for a time, he served as the head golf pro at a local course here in Connecticut. Now he teaches high school in Florida. And coaches their golf team.

22

Inca Dinka Doo

There I was sitting on a block of stone high in the Peruvian Andes. Trying to calm my mind so I could meditate. I had trouble believing that I was actually at the ancient Incan city. Machu Picchu.

Gazing down I could barely make out the train I had gotten off earlier that morning. From my perch at 7,500 ft., it looked like a tiny toy below.

Both the sun and the moon were honored by the Incas. Each was given its own temple at Machu Picchu.

I climbed around them earlier in the day only to be reminded of my horrible fear of heights. I fought off the shaking and weakness in the back of my legs. These Incas didn't believe in handrails.

I was determined not to let my acrophobia ruin this once-in-a-lifetime experience.

As I looked out from my perch high off the ground. I discovered that this was actually a valley, surrounded by much taller mountains. Dwarfing the long-abandoned stone city where I now stood.

I was lightheaded which might have been from the altitude. More than likely, it was from the coca leaves I was chewing. Or the four cups of coca tea I had with breakfast. Ingesting coca helps to ward off altitude sickness.

I had stepped off the plane a day earlier at Cusco. Its altitude is nearly 12,000 feet – twice that of Denver. I felt like a 90-year-old man. I barely made it across the tarmac carrying my knapsack. I also had a pounding headache. And had trouble breathing.

A few cups of coca tea. And I was almost back to my old self.

So, there I was safely tucked into an outcrop of stone. Carved a millennia ago by people who did not possess the tools nor the technology to accomplish this. How the hell did they do that?

This was a mystery I was determined to explore.

My heart attack and near-death experience several years earlier had set me on a metaphysical search seeking universal truths.

Where did we come from? What is our purpose? Where are we going?

I read through most of the New Age Section of Borders Books (before Amazon put them out of business). I inhaled the Old and New Testament. The Koran. The Book of Mormon. And the Egyptian Book of the Dead.

I studied Tibetan Buddhism with The Dalai Lama. Mindfulness meditation with Hindu guru Ram Das. Ancient Jewish mysticism (The Kabala) with orthodox Rabbis. I spun with Whirling Dervishes, followers of the mystic Rumi. And I was named in a sweat lodge ceremony by an Ogalala Sioux medicine man.

I delved into psychic development, past life regressions, channeling, and out-of-body experiences.

I slept under the skies in the Utah desert, on a Hawaiian beach, and in California's High Sierras.

If all that wasn't exhausting enough, I then went down a rabbit hole with an in-depth study of extraterrestrials.

I never cared much for Sci-Fi. I always thought it was silly. Though Spielberg's ET still makes me tear up.

But after attending a three-day conference in Washington on how to deal with extraterrestrials (when, not *if*, they should decide to show up) I did a deep dive into the world of ETs.

I spent a week studying with a woman who channeled an entity from the Pleiades. The seven-sister star cluster, which has served as a cultural and spiritual touchstone in many cultures.

I also traveled to places said to have been visited by aliens. Including Sedona, Maui, and now Machu Picchu. The lost city of the Incas.

Machu Picchu, in the Quechua Indian language, means *old peak* or *old mountain*. It is said that as a mountain wears down over eons of time, its power or energy is consolidated.... pressed inward and downward. This might explain the powerful energy that I felt as I walked around the 150 outcroppings and buildings. Including the ruins of baths, houses, temples, and sanctuaries that comprise Machu Picchu.

Machu Picchu is tucked high in the Andes. It was unknown to the Spaniards who conquered the Incan civilization in search of gold. The city was left largely intact.

Two mysteries remain to this day. How could the Incas move all that stone up 7,500 ft to build it without the use of the wheel? And when, how, and why did these people disappear almost overnight leaving no trace behind?

Most people agree that Machu Picchu served as some kind of astronomical observatory. Its sacred *Intihuatana* stone accurately indicates the two equinoxes. Amazingly, the sun sits directly over that stone twice a year creating no shadows.

I had a feeling that ETs had something to do with this place. And I was determined to find out how.

I had a room in a small hotel that night near the park's entrance. When the tourists left to catch the last train to Cusco – sounds like an old Monkees song, doesn't it? – I had Machu Picchu largely to myself.

The sun began to set. And a full moon ascended to take its place in the darkening sky above.

I got as comfortable as I could sitting on a slab of stone. I closed my eyes. And began a deep breathing exercise to relax. And to alter my state of consciousness.

I silently asked the universe to provide me with the answers to the questions I sought.

A few minutes into this process I had a very strong feeling. I was no longer alone up there. I kept my eyes closed tightly. I clearly felt another being or entity very close to me.

Do I dare open my eyes? For a few moments, I was frozen. Unable to move. Sitting alone at one of the great wonders of the world.

Moments passed slowly. This powerful presence around me did not lessen in its intensity.

I came all these miles for this. So, I reached for whatever strength I had inside myself. And slowly opened my eyes.

It was a moment I will never forget.

I was staring into the face of a large and smelly llama. He snorted at me. As if to say, "*what the hell are you doing on my rock.*" And I began laughing. Uncontrollably.

It was then the Lennon/McCartney lyric came to mind. For in that moment, I was "The Fool on The Hill."

23

— • —

THE NEWS AT 6:00

Explosive diarrhea. Skin rash. Urinary tract infections. Constipation. Arrhythmia. Bloody stool. Projectile vomiting. Kidney failure. And of course, premature death.

Forgive my slight exaggeration. But these are but a small sampling of the warnings quickly spoken at the end of each pharmaceutical commercial sponsoring my evening news.

Thirty-second spots show cheerful men and women in the 50+ demographic having a wonderful time. Dancing in the street. Planting flowers. Hitting a softball. Playing with children. Getting horny.

One little pill is all you need. And your life will be near perfect. That is the promise.

Except for the possibility of acquiring some or all the maladies listed above.

For me, staying informed has grown increasingly depressing.

It has always been tough watching the gloomy stories on the evening news. Horrifying things continue to happen in our world. New technologies have made it possible to bring every awful thing that happens – even in the most remote places on our planet – directly into our homes. Each and every night.

I've come to accept that news remains true to the old adage, *If it bleeds, it leads.* I understand that it is their job to inform. And unfortunately, that information ofttimes transcends the *who, what, why, where, and when* of a story. And devolves into gruesome entertainment.

But my issue is not with the news departments. For the most part, they do their best. And I appreciate the *feel-good* stories that occasionally conclude their newscasts.

Otherwise, we'd all be spending much more time with my old friends, Johnnie, Jack, and José. Whose last names are Walker, Daniels, and Cuervo.

My issue is with the giant pharmaceutical companies hawking their miracle cures.

Each of these mega-drug titans tells their stories in 30-second increments. They hustle an unsuspecting public, telling them that their products create consumer awareness. While empowering patients to take a more active role in their healthcare decisions.

To which I politely and respectfully call *bullshit*.

I believe much of the information is misleading. There is also an inherent conflict of interest with these commercials.

These direct-to-consumer ads address symptoms rather than potential underlying conditions. And they can lead patients to pressure their doctors for prescriptions. In many cases leading them to become overmedicated.

These drug companies spend more than $6 billion per year on television advertising. Trying to convince us that we might have a particular ailment. For which they now have a pill to correct.

These costs are passed along to us in our bloated healthcare system.

Most European countries have stricter regulations on advertising drugs on television. Perhaps that is why television is more watchable over there.

I for one miss those informative and often entertaining commercials.

Can you remember:

"You deserve a break today."

"It's the real thing."

"Where's the beef?"

"I love New York."

"We're number two. We try harder."

"More taste – Less filling."

"The best part of waking up is Folgers in your cup."

If you were around during the Nixon administration (Yeah, the Watergate guy) cigarettes were advertised on what were then our three major networks, ABC, CBS, and NBC. These spots were great fun.

Doctors in white coats, athletes in uniforms, and all kinds of very attractive people lit up a smoke on my television screen. They made smoking look healthy, fun, sexy, and safe.

I couldn't wait to buy my first pack of Marlboro, light up, and enjoy the fantasy of being a cowboy. But who knew from cowboys on 233rd St. in Queens?

I certainly didn't. But if lighting up helped me to become one, I was in!

Finally, our views on smoking evolved. And Nixon signed the bill banning cigarette commercials.

Perhaps someday they will take drug commercials off the air. In the meantime, I'll keep watching the evening news. And the commercials of the happy people dancing and singing the praises of the American pharmaceutical companies. And the drugs that they sell.

And be amazed at how quickly the side effects are read.

Explosive diarrhea anyone?

24

— • —

THE EXPEDITION

What is 17 ½ feet long. Weighs 5,400 lbs. And costs as much as a year at Harvard?

Norma's Ford Expedition.

This is what she drove when we first started dating. This vehicle was a beast. It was huge. It could house a family. Or perhaps a small tribe.

It passed everything on the road but a gas station. Her mileage was in single digits. It was environmentally inappropriate and economically senseless. This behemoth had to go.

She asked me to accompany her to the Ford dealership. Not because I had any knowledge whatsoever about cars. It was that I had a penis.

Being male, I am sorry to say, even in this enlightened age, is often a prerequisite to get a better deal with our local car dealer.

Norma was smart enough to know that back then, a woman alone at the dealership was destined to get ripped off. And so, my penis and I traipsed along. Offering nothing but a Y chromosome. And a pithy sense of humor.

We walked into the showroom and were immediately set upon by three jackals. Posing as car salesmen.

It took a moment for the alpha jackal to exert his dominance. The other two scurried back to their desks to make believe they were on the phone.

Our salesman was Bud. A heavyset guy about my age. He wore a brown sports coat.

His checkered yellow shirt made him look like a NYC taxi with legs. This improbable outfit was accompanied by a long-out-of-style bright red tie.

I've been challenged by color my entire life. So, I am the last person to criticize anyone else's choice of attire. But he also reeked of cigarette smoke. I think you could have gotten cancer simply by standing next to him.

We sat down in his cluttered office. Two things annoyed me right from the start. First, he kept staring at Norma's chest. Lovely as it is, it was inappropriate, to say the least.

And second, he answered each of her questions directly to me. I suppose he assumed that she was an idiot. Big mistake. I was the one who knew nothing about cars.

Norma negotiated a very good deal on the purchase of a smaller SUV. And she got to unload her gigantic vehicle with a trade-in well in excess of the *Blue Book* value.

Who's the idiot now, Bud?

We were supposed to pick up her new car the very next day.

That evening one of us, probably me, suggested that we bid her old vehicle a fond farewell. With a proper send-off. Neither of us had been parking since our teenage years. So, parking it was.

We drove around the dark roads of Simsbury until finally arriving at a quiet and dimly lit office park.

Giggling like horny teenagers we shut the engine. And let our passion take over. Five minutes later a blue light from Simsbury's finest interrupted us.

In Latin, it might be called *sistos publicus interruptus*. But I don't speak Latin.

We were both slightly disheveled. And somewhat unbuttoned. The officer knocked on our window with her flashlight.

By the surprised expression on her face, I could tell she was expecting teenagers. Not people her parents' age.

"You can't do this here. How old are you? For God sake get a room!" she said in a reprimanding tone.

And then she smiled. Knowing that she had a funny story to take back to the stationhouse. In a town where almost nothing happens on the night shift.

I like making people laugh.

Norma picked up her new car the next morning. And of course, Bud asked her out on a date.

25

— • —

A LADLE OF LOVE

There are those nights when the digital clock on my nightstand reminds me of each hour that I am not sleeping.

It is in those hours my mind is a mosh pit of half-formed thoughts. Trying to sort all that is happening in my life. After I've tossed and turned for an hour or so. I surrender and just get up.

The house is quiet. I leave the room without disturbing my wife who remains blissfully in dream land.

On warm nights I take refuge on the deck in the rear of my house. I drop myself down on my chaise. To visit my old friend. The night sky.

The fact that I can identify only a handful of celestial objects by name does nothing to diminish the wondrous show they put on night after night.

I have often thought of setting up a telescope. But I know that it will eventually end up laughing at me. As it collects dust with a closet full of my other initially well-intentioned but ultimately little-used contraptions.

So, I quietly sit.

My view is of the northern sky. The largest object I can spot is the Big Dipper. The seven brightest stars in Ursa Major. Easy to see with the naked eye.

Through millennia it has been used for navigation. If you can find the Big Dipper and the nearby North Star, you can navigate your way home. In the desert. The mountains. Or on the high seas.

It was the North Star the Three Kings followed to the manger at the birth of Jesus.

And it was the Big Dipper that served as a coded message to help enslaved people escape to the North in pre-Civil War America.

The African American spiritual "Follow the Drinking Gourd" contained directions and encouragement in its song lyrics. And served as a symbol of hope and guidance for a better life.

The Big Dipper has been a reliable touchstone my entire life. I often think about it holding the wisdom of the ages as it points north. Keeping me on my path.

Now and again my thoughts go to an unknown guy living sometime in the Middle Ages. How he toiled each day to feed his family and survive the challenges of his time.

How in quiet moments, perhaps under this very cluster of stars, he dreamt of a world outside of his village. Perhaps on the other side of a mountain. Or to the furthest part of the yet-to-be-explored ocean.

What would he think of us today? We live in a world with flying machines and submarines. With medicines to cure the diseases that ravaged his village.

We have the ability to communicate with each other around the globe. Sharing our knowledge through books, broadcasts and satellites. In a world connected through handheld devices.

As I sit on my deck, gazing at the star-filled night, I think that guy is a lot like me. What will the future bring, I muse? With knowledge expanding exponentially, what new devices and inventions will someday be commonplace?

I won't live to see mankind explore or for that matter settle on other planets or in other galaxies. Perhaps the children of my grandchildren will.

But a larger question looms. Like the sword of Damocles dangling perilously above us.

Are we capable of evolving into a better species? Can we begin taking care of each other on the planet we share? Can we become good stewards of the land we borrow from our children?

I certainly don't know. And I don't claim to have the answers. Frankly, I don't really trust anyone who does.

I've resolved to improve the world by improving myself. Living my life in peace and love. In hopes that it is contagious.

In troubling times when I am distracted by worries and fears. All I need to do is look up. Recalibrate. And navigate my way home.

26

— • —

LITTLE NUGGETS

The following are some little nuggets. Small stories. Things that happened along the way. Not long enough to merit a full chapter. But they are amusing. I'm guessing that you've had some of these same experiences. Or perhaps you will.

Grocery Shopping

One afternoon some years ago I stopped to pick up a few groceries. There was a woman in front of me in the check-out line. She was a bit frazzled. Her child was in the grocery cart seat. Throwing a tantrum. Upset that his mom would not buy something he wanted.

Her groceries totaled a little less than $50. She reached into her purse but couldn't find her wallet. Now she started to melt down along with her 2-year-old. That is when I stepped in.

"Let me help you out here," I said. *"You take care of your child and I'll pay for the groceries."*

She seemed relieved and thanked me profusely. She said she would pay me back when she got home. I gave her my card so she could drop a check in the mail.

I had been struggling financially so $50 was not an inconsequential amount of money to me. But I was raised right. And doing the right thing has always been important to me.

I felt good about myself. As I walked out of the store with my bag of groceries in hand, I saw her drive away in her shiny new Lexus.

I shrugged my shoulders and headed home in my 5-year-old Subaru.

Her check never arrived.

Clan Chowder

Between us, Norma and I have four children. Jason (Jay) and Jonathan (Jon) are mine. Alexandra (Alex) and Andrew (Drew) are Norma's. As you can see, each of them goes through life with a shortened name. But that is the only thing short about them.

End to end they measure 24 ½ feet. Combined they have 10 degrees. With a shared IQ somewhere in the high 500s. Simply put, they are tall and smart. Each possesses a healthy sense of humor. And put up with Norma and me without too much eye-rolling.

We don't use the word *Step* in our house. We treat our four children equally as if we were the birth parents of each. I am Grandpa to the four grandchildren. And Norma is Abu, which is short for Abuela – grandmother in Spanish.

We are so lucky to have a family that truly enjoys each other's company. Our kids along with Amy's children and Tom's son are part of a group they call *the Cousins Club*. Our grandkids have become *the Cousins Club 2.0*.

We are a big, squishy, hugging, loving family. When we are together, it is a party. Full of laughter and joy.

Now I'm not saying that we are perfect. We certainly are not. From time to time we can get on each other's nerves. I'm told I can be quite annoying. But the love we have for each other overpowers the quirky idiosyncrasies that make us who we are.

I have friends whose family members simply don't like each other. They go through life dreading family gatherings of every kind. And that makes me sad.

I believe that stress and heartache can be passed on to future generations. But so too can caring and loving.

We put a lot of energy into nurturing our family relationships.

And the wonderful dividends continue to pay off.

The Most Wrong I Ever Was

Sometime in the 1980's I had lunch with a client whose brother was putting together an IPO (initial public offering) for a company that sold home improvement products in the South. He asked me if I wanted to invest.

"Who would ever shop at a 100,000 sq. ft. hardware store? That's the dumbest idea I have ever heard," I said confidently.

Home Depot now operates more than 2,300 stores and has annual sales of over $150 billion. It was the most wrong I've ever been.

Out of Africa

The cab driver who picked me up at the Las Vegas airport asked me where I was from. I told him I grew up in NY and now lived in Connecticut.

"There are a lot of Jews in New York City," he said. More of a question than a statement. In my attempt to change the subject, I asked him where he was from.

"Ethiopia. I've been in the US for two years. Are you a Jewish man?" he asked.

His question annoyed me to no end. Too personal. Nevertheless, I said, *"Yes, I am. Do you have a problem with that?"*

"Oh, no sir. I am also a Jew. It's just that you don't look Jewish," he said flashing a broad smile.

I then realized that this Black man driving my cab was an Ethiopian Jew. To him, I certainly didn't look Jewish. I'm a white guy.

The Jews of Ethiopia are thought to be descendants of King Solomon and the Queen of Sheba. I remember reading about their very long and interesting history. There are some 160,000 Ethiopian Jews today in Israel.

As I shook his hand, tipping him generously, I noticed he wore a Star of David. I said *"Shalom, my friend."*

You never can tell who you are going to meet in Las Vegas.

Flying with the King

I took the afternoon flight from Las Vegas to Chicago. My seatmate was Elvis. No, not the guy buried at Graceland. This was a professional Elvis impersonator.

During our 2-hour flight he never once broke character. I was indeed, chatting with Elvis. And he was delightful. Perhaps a little crazy. But still delightful.

We parted company to each catch our connecting flights home. I told him it was a pleasure chatting with him. And I wished him well.

In his basso voice, he simply said, *"Thank you very much. Elvis has left the plane."*

My Friend from Cairo

A friend of mine has a most unusual background. He is an Egyptian Jew. Who grew up in Cairo. He was there during the Six-Day War of 1967. And the Yom Kippur War of 1973. He then came to the US to attend college.

I found this absolutely fascinating. He said he lived in the Greek section of Cairo and was never bothered by the Egyptians.

"So you and your family celebrated all of the Jewish holidays there?" I asked.

"Yes. My parents belonged to a synagogue in Cairo. Though it was pretty low profile," he said.

"How did you celebrate Passover? Moses led our people out of Egypt to the promised land. But you guys were still there," I said.

"I've been living in the US for my entire adult life, and no one ever asked me that. You are such a pain in the ass. I suppose that is why we are friends," he responded with a smile.

A Grande Latte

Most things show up in Connecticut long after they are commonplace elsewhere. I was a little baffled when Starbucks finally opened here.

I walked up to the counter and asked for a coffee from the young heavily tattooed barista. Up until then, I had thought that a barista was an English lawyer with a wig. Her eyes rolled and she explained that she was a barista. Not a barrister.

She then asked whether my coffee would be Tall. Grande. Or Venti.

It turns out that *Tall* means small. And that *Grande*, which is Italian for large – actually is a medium. And *Venti* which means twenty in Italian is their big size. Who knew?

Confused, I shrugged my shoulders and asked her for three bucks worth.

Norma and I often find ourselves in Starbucks. The barista takes our order. And asks for our names to be written on the cups.

Fred and Wilma are the names I like to use. Norma prefers Ferdinand and Isabella. Everyone in the coffee shop over 40 is delighted when our names are called by an unsuspecting and overworked barista.

I Love Italy

My fluency in Italian is strictly limited to Italian restaurant menus. And maybe finding a bathroom. That is about as far as my language skills take me.

Norma and I were in Italy. Florence to be specific. We stopped into a nice café. While she went to the restroom, I was charged with ordering us a couple of coffees. Nice big lattes to perk us up as we would soon be headed to yet another museum.

My feet hurt. I was cranky. And I was looking forward to sitting down and re-caffeinating.

I bellied up to the coffee bar and ordered with my very best Italian accent *"due latte, per favore"*.... asking the barista for two hot lattes. I even held up two fingers to be clear.

He gave me a snarky look and pushed a few buttons on the enormous espresso machine. After the machine stopped hissing, he served me two cups of hot milk. And once again gave me his snarky smile.

Rather than giving in to my embarrassment I simply ordered *"Due espressi, per favore."*

I poured the two espressos into the two cups of hot milk. And smiled snarkily right back at him.

Although it cost me twice as much, it was still cheaper than a couple of Grande Lattes at our Starbuck's back home.

To foster good international relations, I left him an unnecessarily generous tip.

AMO L'ITALIA.

When the Shoe is on the Other Foot

During my real estate career, I had the pleasure of leasing to numerous retail businesses within the Asian community. On one occasion I asked the owner of a large Asian grocery store if she had seen my client. The owner of the shopping plaza.

She had known both of us for more than a year.

His name is Rick. He has blond hair and is clean-shaven. He is 15 years younger than me. My name is Eric. I am six inches taller and 20 lbs. heavier than him. I have brown hair and a mustache.

"I don't know. You people all look the same to me," she said.

The Dinner Party

My wife and I arrived late at the home of my boss. It was my first holiday dinner party. I was the new guy in the ad agency. I was twenty-four. And I was nervous.

We were greeted at the door by my boss, his wife, and their little white Bichon Frise named Rufus. I'm not a big fan of *man's best friend.* I've got enough friends. This one looked like a snowball with teeth.

As they took our coats Rufus proceeded to hump my wife's leg.

Before I could disengage my mouth, I said *"Tell him you have a headache."*

If looks could kill, they would have called the county coroner. One more nail in the coffin that was my first marriage.

When the FBI Wrote back

When the 'Freedom of Information Act" was passed in the late 1970s, I wrote to the FBI asking for a copy of my file. I had been active in the anti-war movement as a college student. Therefore it was reasonable to assume there might be a file on me. And I wanted to read it.

Months later their response came, in an official-looking envelope with a return address of the FBI office in Washington.

That very day I had seriously jammed my ring finger playing basketball. I thought it might be broken.

On the way to the refrigerator to grab some ice for my finger, I tossed the mail on the kitchen table. I never looked at it.

With the help of some butter, I managed to get my wedding ring off my swollen finger. I tossed the ring on the kitchen table, too. And I scooted out the door to the emergency room for an X-ray.

In those days there were no urgent care centers. Or, for that matter, cell phones. And the waiting time for a simple X-ray was several hours.

When my wife came home, she saw my wedding ring on the table. Along with the letter from the FBI which she was afraid to open.

Under normal circumstances, my first wife was not a calm woman. By the time I returned home some five hours later, she had pretty much lost her mind. Imagining all sorts of horrible scenarios.

Yeah, I probably should have left a note.

27

— • —

THINGS THAT GO BUMP

I t was 3 o'clock in the morning. I had been sound asleep. The headlights from a passing car danced across my bedroom ceiling. And then I heard a car door close.

We live on a quiet suburban street. Nothing much happens here. Particularly in the middle of the night.

I assumed that the activity had something to do with my neighbors. They were expecting their second child at any time.

As I started to fall back asleep, I heard what sounded like footsteps in my house. It wasn't Norma. In the glow from our clock radio, I could see her on the other side of our king-sized bed. She was deep in dreamland. Blissfully purring away.

We have no animals. And our kids have been out in their own lives for years. The noise was not theirs.

I listened carefully. There was definitely someone downstairs. I was now on high alert. And getting really angry.

I have lived in this house for over forty years. And only recently began locking my door. How dare someone disrupt the sanctity of my home? There will be consequences!

Our neighborhood often has power outages. So, I keep a large flashlight on my nightstand. It illuminates a very bright and wide arc of light.

The eighteen-inch, solidly constructed mag light contains four D-cell batteries. And weighs a couple of pounds. It is as much a weapon as it is a flashlight.

I got out of bed and quietly reached for the flashlight. The noise continued from downstairs. Clearly there was someone in my house. This pissed me off to no end.

Taking small footsteps, I walked from my bedroom to the top of the stairs. I was barefoot. Wearing nothing but my jockey shorts. Nevertheless, I was going to kick someone's ass for breaking into my home.

Had a saner moment prevailed I would have called 911. Simsbury's finest would have dropped their late-night donuts. And been here with guns drawn in no time flat.

Frankly, I never even thought of calling them. In that moment, I was far from sane.

I slowly walked down the steps. Remembering that you can be pretty much squeak-free if your footsteps are taken on the widest edges of each step.

Finally, I made my way down the stairs. I was sure the intruder didn't hear me because he was still rummaging through my living room.

I took a couple of slow breaths to calm my nerves. I was going to clock this son of a bitch with my giant flashlight.

"You're a dead man, motherfucker!" I shouted as I spun into the room.

I froze mid-sentence. For in front of me was a sight I will not soon forget.

We own a Roomba. Which vacuums the floors of our house with the push of a button.

One of us must have accidentally set the timer. Because Rosie, the name we gave it as a homage to The Jetsons, was rolling around vacuuming our house. At three o'clock in the morning.

I was relieved that I didn't get to clock a burglar. Had I busted open his head there would have been sirens, lights, an ambulance, police, and a ton of paperwork.

He also could have been a martial arts guy and knocked me on my ass. In either event, there would have been angst, stress, blood, and a fair amount of yelling and tears.

I was glad to just shut Rosie down. Extinguish the light in my killer flashlight. And crawl back into bed wondering if I should tell Norma about this in the morning.

I did. She laughed. And then she got pissed at me for not calling 911. I married a woman who is smarter than me.

If there is a next time, I am going to call 911. And if the police come and shoot Rosie in my living room, I'll have a good story for my next book.

28

DOWN AND OUT

He was a hulk of a man. A couple of decades earlier he might have been a linebacker on a college football team. He certainly had the size.

He was dressed in a ragged jacket. Just thick enough to keep the cold autumn breeze from chilling his bones. His belongings were packed away in the small grocery cart he pushed along the sidewalk.

People kept their distance. They gave him a wide berth as he passed by. Their body language revealed they were afraid of him. At first, I thought they feared his imposing size. But upon further reflection, I believe it was his homelessness they feared.

Perhaps it was their own anxiety bubbling up to the surface. *There but for the grace of God go I* – I could almost hear them say as I read their faces.

To be honest I did calculate a few times how many paychecks I'd have to miss before ending up as one of the faceless, homeless people.

But I was employed. I had a first-floor office in a building next to the train station in Hartford. It was within eyeshot of the State Capitol on the opposite side of Bushnell Park. Not the best of neighborhoods.

Most mornings I'd be sitting at my desk by the window sipping my first cup of coffee. Reading the newspaper. Getting ready to start my day.

With a gentle suddenness, there would be a knock at my window. And there he was. All 300 lbs. of him.

He would give me a quick smile. And a slight nod of his head. And then burst into song. An operatic melody in his powerful tenor's voice.

He'd clearly had musical training. Perhaps as a younger man, he studied at the nearby Hartt College of Music. At the time, I was not much of an opera aficionado. But even I could recognize *Nessun Dorma* from Turandot.

He'd finish his aria. I'd put my coffee down and applaud. And he'd continue his stroll toward Bushnell Park. Whenever I'd see him walking the neighborhood, I would thank him for his gift of music. And give him a couple of dollars.

I wanted to tell him that this was not a handout. It was payment for making my mornings so delightful. But before I could, he just turned his back to me. And shuffled away.

Now and then I still think about how he ended up on the streets. And I wonder what became of him. The saddest person I'd ever seen singing the most beautiful passages I'd ever heard.

That Thanksgiving I found myself alone. My children went with their mother to visit her family. I could have driven to NY to be with my family. Or invited myself to a friend's home. But I was feeling depressed.

I've found that doing something for someone else always chases my blues away.

I called a local shelter to ask if I could help with their Thanksgiving meal. They were delighted to have another pair of hands.

It was a large shelter. There were more than 20 volunteers that day. Setting out meals for a very long line of folks who needed and appreciated a turkey dinner with all the trimmings.

Being of service to others made me feel so much better. I spent a beautiful day with sweet and generous people. On both sides of the serving table.

Unbeknownst to me there was a photographer.

The next morning my photo was on the front page of The Hartford Courant, serving Thanksgiving dinner.

I was embarrassed and quite annoyed at this. I did a one-day pop-in. Others who show up day in and day out should have gotten the recognition they deserved. I never asked for nor wanted the exposure.

However, I received a number of calls in the days that followed. Many of my friends and business associates asked how they could help at the shelter.

Each time I passed along the contact information I felt more positive about the photo. I am always happily surprised at how a small act of kindness can have more far-reaching results.

Years later we got hit with an extraordinary mid-October snowstorm. It was dubbed *Snowtober*.

The power was out in most of our town for a couple of weeks. No heat. No lights. Each day became increasingly more challenging.

On day four we got word that the high school had power. We headed there to get our phones and laptops charged. The gymnasium had cots if we needed a warm place to sleep. There were also a couple of large pots of soup for all who were there.

So there I was in the middle of a wealthy community. Standing in a soup line. I had not showered, shaved, or had a warm meal for several days. Soup never tasted more comforting.

Friends who lived in other towns and had power invited us over for showers. And a warm meal. It was a new experience for me having to rely on the kindness of others.

My thoughts went to the poor and the homeless who are not as fortunate. It took some time, but everything eventually got back to normal.

And I am happy that each year I am able to contribute toward helping others. Remembering that I remain one bad weather event away from standing in a soup line.

29

— • —

THE WAY

El Camino de Santiago is a network of pilgrimage routes, leading to the apostle Saint James the Great's tomb. In the Cathedral of Santiago de Compostela in Galicia. In northwestern Spain.

The Pilgrimage, which dates to the early 9th century has been an important Christian tradition for well over a thousand years.

The journey is hundreds of miles long.

The destination is the architectural and spiritually significant marvel – the gigantic Cathedral of St. James. It was founded in the year 821. Just as a point of reference, that was about a thousand years before the time of Thomas Jefferson.

The Camino de Santiago is for serious hikers. It can take a month or more to finish. Though many take shorter, less intense walks.

Norma and I took this journey. Our pilgrimage was 460 miles. Starting at San Sebastian near the French border in Spain's Basque region. Right across the top of Spain along the Bay of Biscay, to its very end at Cape Finisterre and the Atlantic Ocean.

It was a two-week journey with a dozen overnights. Allowing us time to explore the cultural diversity of the region.

You might ask how two senior citizens could cover that distance in two weeks. And still have time to explore the area?

I'd like to tell you we walked fast. Truth be told – we did it by bus.

Had we been a decade or two younger we might have tried to hoof a portion of it. But at our age, we thought the better of it.

The Camino is a path that takes you inward. Each of the countless thousands of steps brings one to a higher consciousness. And to the God as you imagine it to be.

Of course, there are some on the road who look at The Camino as a physical challenge to be conquered. Like climbing a mountain. Or running with the bulls at Pamplona. A bit like exercising one's ego. Making it about bragging rights.

But for the most part. This is a solemn pilgrimage. An inward adventure. To connect with *your own* higher self.

At the entrance to the enormous Cathedral of St. James one sees weary pilgrims trudging with their backpacks and walking sticks.

They are near exhaustion. With blistered feet and achy bones. In need of a warm bath, and a comfortable bed. But the gleam in their eyes tells a more complete story.

It is a look of ecstasy. For somewhere along their journey they found what they came for. A sense of belonging and connection.

Each pilgrim has a story to tell. About the kindness of strangers. Sleeping under the stars or in hostels. And breaking bread with like-minded travelers from around the world. Wishing each other *Buen Camino* – a good walk.

Just as it has been since the Middle Ages.

Norma and I have traveled to many parts of Spain. Wherever we've gone I've felt immediately at home. The sounds. The tastes. The smells. All have a visceral effect on me. As though I've been here before.

Spain is a wonderfully diverse country. With a long and complicated history. It is comprised of 16 autonomous regions. Each with its own distinctive culture, history, cuisine – and in some cases language.

Over the years several of these regions pressed for their independence from Spain. Claiming a stronger identity with their regional cultures. Thus far, Spain has held together.

I have come to appreciate the beauty as well as the architectural and spiritual significance of the gigantic gold-filled cathedrals found throughout the country. But being a Jewish guy I find myself conflicted.

As I begin to understand the Catholic Church and its influences on Spain, I remain appalled at the distressing years of The Inquisition. A time when Jews either accepted the teachings of the Church – or died a horrific death.

Walking through the old Jewish quarters of many Spanish cities including Barcelona, Seville, Girona, Toledo, Segovia and Cordoba, a strange thing happened.

I felt powerfully drawn to these places. Like I had been there already. It was an odd sense of déjà vu I had never experienced before. And couldn't explain.

For centuries Jews, Muslims (Moors), and Catholics peacefully coexisted. Then in 1492 Ferdinand and Isabella issued the Alhambra Decree. Mandating the expulsion of Jews from Spain.

My grandparents emigrated through Ellis Island from the Ukraine (then a part of Russia) in the early 1900s. A typical American story.

We knew little about my ancestor's time in Europe. My guess had always been that they lived for a time in Spain. Before being forced out around the time of the Inquisition.

I assumed they then found their way across Europe to the Ukraine where they lived for generations. Only to be driven out once again to the US early in the 20th century.

All that, of course, was just speculation on my part. That is until I spit in a tube. And a DNA test proved this out.

I was able to trace my family over 58 generations. From the Middle East through Turkey and into Europe. Where they did, indeed, live in Spain for hundreds of years.

So somewhere in the medieval cities of Spain, I found *My Way*. My very own *Camino*. My path to reflect. In a place my ancestors called home so many centuries ago.

Encontré Mi Camino.

AFTERWORD

This is the third book of stories from my life.

To be honest, I never thought I'd have enough material to fill one book. Let alone three. Yet here we are. Some 90 stories later.

As I sit down to write these final words, I am filled with a profound sense of gratitude. To each and every one of you who has turned the pages of my life. I thank you.

Writing these stories has been both a challenge and a privilege. It has required me to confront the ghosts of my past. And sift through memories both painful and joyous.

From time to time I am approached by one of my readers. Telling me how much they've enjoyed my stories. For this, I am truly humbled.

Through my writing, I've learned that life stories and experiences are meant to be shared. I am reminded that storytelling has the power to heal. To inspire. And to unite us in our shared humanity.

Initially, my goal was a simple one. To write a few stories for my grand-kids. About the people who came before them. I was missing my parents and grandparents. Writing about them and the simpler days of my child-hood and adolescence gave me the opportunity to revisit parts of my life.

As I wrote I discovered I had more to say. And that my words might encourage others to take their own pen to paper. To share stories about their lives with those most important to them.

To my readers, I encourage you to continue your own journeys of self-discovery and personal growth. It is my sincere hope that my stories may serve as a reminder that no matter how rocky the road may seem, there is beauty and joy to be found in the journey.

May we all find the courage to embrace our truths. To celebrate our victories. And to navigate life's twists and turns with grace and resilience.

Thank you for allowing me to share my stories.

Much love,

Eric Litsky

Simsbury, CT

Let's stay in touch.

www.EricLitsky.com

— · —

Acknowledgements

I would like to express my love and sincere gratitude to my wife Norma for her unwavering support and encouragement in completing this book. And to her gently nudging me to return to my laptop each time I thought I was done. Which was often.

I am deeply thankful to my brother Andy. He continues to remind me of the little details of the life we shared as children. Though we spent our early years beating the hell out of each other as brothers often do. The only thing we now fight about is how I often mangle the English language. And ignore the conventions of grammar and punctuation.

I am indebted to Colleen Brunetti of Bannon River Books for her constructive feedback and insightful suggestions as this book began to take shape. And her skills at coordinating the details to bring it to publication.

My heartfelt appreciation goes to Laura English of Evergreen Studios who directed and produced the audio version of this book.

I would also like to thank Arlene Soto of Intricate Designs whose artistic hands prove that you can judge a book by its cover.

Finally, I would like to express my gratitude to my friends and family for their continuous support. And for unwittingly being the inspiration for many of my stories.

ABOUT THE AUTHOR

Eric Litsky was born in the Bronx and raised in Queens in the middle of the post-war, baby boom years. After his tumultuous college years, he had a 10-year career in advertising/public relations followed by three decades as a commercial real estate broker.

Between his careers and raising a family, Litsky has been an amateur singer/songwriter, tango dancer, stage actor, musician (tuba player) and now an author.

He resides with his wife Norma in Northern Connecticut

www.ingramcontent.com/pod-product-compliance
Lightning Source LLC
Chambersburg PA
CBHW051212120626
46547CB00013B/1311